# THE
# RESURRECTION
# OF
# JESUS

# THE
# RESURRECTION
# OF JESUS

## Gary R. Habermas

UNIVERSITY
PRESS OF
AMERICA

LANHAM • NEW YORK • LONDON

Copyright © 1984 by

University Press of America,™ Inc.

4720 Boston Way
Lanham, MD 20706

3 Henrietta Street
London WC2E 8LU England

ISBN (Perfect): 0-8191-3750-2

Originally published by
Baker Book House in 1980.

**To Debbie**

My love,
my closest earthly friend,
and my wife.

Special acknowledgments should be made to several for assistance in the publication of this book. Permission to quote copyrighted material was granted by several publishing companies, as follows:

Macmillan Publishing Co., Inc. for quotes from *Miracles* by C. L. Lewis, copyright 1947 and from *The Cost of Discipleship* by Dietrich Bonhoeffer (Second Edition), copyright SCM Press Ltd., 1959. Used by permission.
Zondervan Publishing House for material from *Philosophy of Religion* by Norman Geisler, copyright 1974 by The Zondervan Corporation. Used by permission.
David C. Cook Publishing Co. for material from *The View From a Hearse* by Joseph Bayly, copyright 1969. Used by permission
Baker Book House for material from *Christian Apologetics* by Norman Geisler, copyright 1976. Used by permission.

Special thanks is also extended to Montana Institute of the Bible for graciously granting permission for the time to write the main draft for this book in the summer of 1978 and to Harold L. Longenecker, then the President, for reading the manuscript and for offering much encouragement.

Additionally, I would also like to thank Norman Geisler for reading the manuscript, for offering valuable suggestions and especially for writing the Foreword.

Special thanks should also be directed to Baker Book House, and to Peter Schneider in particular, for reviewing the manuscript and for publishing it.

Lastly, I would like to acknowledge the faithful assistance of my wife Debbie, who willingly performed the chore of typing this material.

Gary R. Habermas
March, 1980

# Foreword

Christian apologetics has three great tasks: reasoning for the existence of God, establishing the deity of Christ, and defending the inspiration of Scripture. In this book Dr. Habermas has related each of these three tasks to the historical kingpin of the Christian faith—the resurrection of Jesus Christ.

This work can be termed a "resurrection apologetic" in two different senses. First, the author considers the resurrection to be the single most crucial element of Christian apologetics. Second, other key aspects of the Christian faith are related to the central fact of the resurrection, including the existence of God, the deity of Christ, the inspiration of the Bible, and the assurance of eternal life.

Although Dr. Habermas handles his subject with philosophical sophistication, this book can be appreciated by the layman as well as the scholar. *The Resurrection of Jesus: An Apologetic* signals the growing number of younger evangelical scholars who are attacking head-on the historical scepticism of David Hume and the philosophical agnosticism of Immanuel Kant.

What distinguishes this work from the usual historical apologetic is that Dr. Habermas has taken seriously the need to set his resurrection apologetic within the broader context of a rational theism. A purely historical apologetic lacking this dimension seems crucially inadequate. Therefore, this book, despite its brevity, makes a significant contribution to this new impetus in Christian apologetics.

NORMAN GEISLER

# Contents

# Introduction

Many Christians know that the resurrection of Jesus is the center of the Christian faith, but few realize exactly how it provides this center. It is the purpose of this book to establish the resurrection as the foundation of both Christian theology as a whole and apologetics in particular. Our endeavor will be to show how such a basis is furnished by the historicity of this event.

## The Center of Christian Apologetics and Theology

It is the testimony of the New Testament that the resurrection of Jesus is the absolute center of the Christian faith. This is also affirmed by the vast majority of scholars today, both conservative and liberal.

The key passage in this regard is I Cor. 15. After citing an early Christian creed which provides a list of appearances of the resurrected Jesus (vv. 3ff.), Paul turns to the significance of the resurrection in verse 12.

Paul states that if Jesus was not raised from the dead, then the Christian faith and preaching are necessarily fallacious (Greek κενός). Thus the apostles, who were eyewitnesses to the appearances (vv. 11, 14, 15), must be lying by affirming that God raised Jesus (vv. 14-15).

Again Paul emphasizes that the entire Christian faith is ineffective (Greek μάτιος) when considered apart from Jesus' literal resurrection. As a direct result, there is no forgiveness of sins, which means that all believers who have died have perished in vain (vv. 17-18).

Without the fact of the resurrection, our only hope lies in this life. Because our hope would only be of this mundane variety, we would be the most pitied of all men (v. 19). We would be living a lie.

After outlining this dismal picture of a spineless Christianity, Paul concludes on a triumphant note. Christ *was* raised from the dead (v. 20), therefore providing a firm foundation for our faith.

We can now reserve the doubts raised earlier. Christianity thus teaches the truth and no one proclaiming Christ is lying (vv. 14, 15). We now have a ground for claiming the forgiveness of sins (v. 17), and those who have died in Christ do have eternal life (v. 18). Therefore, this life does have much meaning, based on our future (v. 19).

Jesus' death and ressurection (v. 3, 4) therefore becomes the basis for the validity of Christian theology, according to Paul in I Cor. 15:12-20. Indeed, without it there would be no faith at all. From this foundation, Paul goes on to develop the doctrine of the resurrection of the body (vv. 20-58).

By no means is I Cor. 15 the only witness of the early church to the centrality of Jesus' resurrection. In Romans 1:3, 4 Paul cites another ancient creed which relates a brief Christology. Jesus is asserted to be both God's Son and the seed of David (v. 3). Paul declares that Jesus was demonstrated to be both the Son of God and Lord by His resurrection from the dead (v. 4). Thus this event becomes the chief evidence for the Person of Christ.

The Book of Acts relates several discourses in which the resurrection is the prima facie evidence for the theology which is being proclaimed. In Acts 2:22-24, Luke relates that Peter's first message used Jesus' being raised by God as the attestation of Jesus' Person. Thus, in order to convince unbelieving Jews of the veracity of Christ, Peter referred to the resurrection as the chief evidence.

Acts 13:26-39 contains a sermon by Paul in which he challenges the people of Antioch. An elaboration of the resurrection (vv. 28-37) provides the basis for his plea for those present to respond to salvation through Christ, which calls for repentance of sin and the exercise of faith (vv. 38-39).

Probably the best example in Acts where the resurrection is cited as the basis of Christian theology is found in Paul's Aeropagus lecture (17:22-34). Paul begins by speaking of God's existence and by recounting some of His acts, such as creation (vv. 22-29). Turning to the point of his message, Paul tells of God's call to all men to repent in light of the coming judgment in which Christ will act as Judge. Paul concludes that God has given a guarantee (Greek πίστις) of the truthfulness of all of these doctrines by raising Jesus from the dead. Thus, God's call, the need for repentance, the coming judgment, and the work of Christ are all said to be verified by the resurrection (v. 30, 31).

Other parts of the New Testament also utilize the resurrection as the chief basis for Christian theology. In Romans 10:9 the early Christological formula "Jesus is Lord" and salvation rest on God's raising Jesus from the dead. The resurrection also reveals Christ's Lordship (Rom. 14:9) and provides a basis for the future resurrection and eternal life of the believer (II Cor. 14:4; I Thess. 4:14).

Still other instances could be cited, but these examples are sufficient to show that in the early church, the resurrection was the chief basis for Christian theology. Doctrines were said to have been demonstrated by the reality of this historical event. In addition, defenses of the faith were based on the resurrection (I Cor. 15:3-20; Acts 2:22-24; 17:30-31), thus making it the center of apologetics. In brief, without this event there would be no theology or apologetics at all.

## The Relevance of the Resurrection Today

Thus it is my conviction that the resurrection continues to provide a strong foundation for Christian theology. This particularly applies to apologetics. However, a warning should be given at this point. It is *not* my purpose to assert either explicitly or implicitly that the resurrection is the exclusive basis for Christian apologetics. Many other evidences corroborate the truthfulness of Christian theology, such as fulfilled prophecy. Neither should the resurrection be arbitrarily separated from these other evidences. Therefore, in this work we are concentrating on the special significance of this event for apologetics without claiming that it is the only approach to this subject or that it should be isolated from other apologetic endeavors.

My approach in this book will be to build a modest apologetic system around the resurrection. This effort will endeavor to give an example of how this event may serve as a foundation for the Christian faith.

Briefly, the apologetic is composed of five major points. The first step will demonstrate the validity of the literal resurrection of Jesus. An apologetic for its historicity will be provided, based on several key points. It is my contention that even by skeptical standards, this event can be demonstrated to be true.

Second, I will present a basis for the existence and activity of God, who was particularly manifested in His raising of Jesus. Third, I will show that by raising Jesus from the dead, God approved and vindicated Jesus' entire message concerning both His own Person and His other teachings.

Jesus' central teaching concerning the Kingdom of God and the entrance requirements of salvation is the next area of concentration. Specifically, we will be concerned, fourth, with this concept of Kingdom while, fifth, we will investigate the personal decision of salvation which Jesus called men to make in order to enter the eternal life of God's Kingdom.

One chapter is given to the development of each of these five major points. These five chapters are followed by several appendices which explicate specific points of integral interest. These appendices cover such topics as the resurrection as a critique of world views, the inspiration of Scripture, the reality of eternal life, and the place of the Holy Spirit in apologetic reasoning.

It is not being claimed that this apologetic system is completely unique, although this author is not aware of anything very similar. This five point system was developed several years ago by the author and it has been "tested" in many lectures both in the classroom and in other conferences ever since that time.

Neither is there any claim being made that this is the best apologetic system available. It should definitely be used in conjunction with other approaches in order to facilitate the widest possible proclamation of Christian truth. We will turn now to the context in which such a system might work the best.

## The Use of this Apologetic System

In the New Testament, one had to use a variety of approaches in presenting the truth of Christ to the people because of the different orientations and personalities of the audiences. Many times a straightforward presentation of the gospel was just what was needed. This is shown in Jesus' session with Nicodemus (John 3:1ff.) and with the woman at the well (John 4:5ff.). Similar instances are Peter's visit with Cornelius (Acts 10:34-48), the testimony of Paul and his company to Lydia (Acts 16:13-15) and the witness of Paul and Silas to the Philippian jailer (Acts 16:23-34).

However, other times it was only by being given evidences and the logical reasoning behind the truths of Christianity that people were persuaded by the Holy Spirit to accept the gospel. Examples of this would be Paul's visits to Thessalonica (Acts 17:1-4), Areopagus (Acts 17:22-34), Corinth (Acts 18:4) and Ephesus (Acts 19:8-10). These instances indicate that reasoning concerning the evidence presented for the gospel was a method sometimes used to win many to Christ.

It is obvious even from this brief overview that the Holy Spirit used various techniques in communicating the gospel to men. It is my contention that various methods need to be used even today to explain and defend Christian truth. (A more indepth explanation of the relationship between the Holy Spirit and apologetic methodology is presented in Appendix 4.)

This apologetic system is not to be considered in any way as an exclusive means of presenting the gospel. Oftentimes a straightforward testimony or other presentation of the gospel is exactly what is needed. The system contained herein would be most useful when a more evidential approach is needed.

This system might be used in two ways. First, there is the real possibility that believers might be strengthened in their faith by a presentation of Christianity's strong foundation. Hence, it might be used to strengthen one's own faith.

Second, this apologetic has also been developed to confront the skeptic with the rationality of the Christian faith. To this end, various arguments have been elaborated here even for skeptics who reject not only the Christian faith, but who also reject such starting places as the Scriptures or even God's existence. One example of this is in the first chapter on Jesus' resurrection. As Paul demonstrated at Areopagus (Acts 17:22-34), even such harsh skeptics can also be successfully presented with the gospel.

Therefore, the key to the use of such a system is the leading of the Holy Spirit with respect to the needs of the person in question. Without the leading of the Spirit in the unbeliever's life, no one will genuinely be convinced anyway. Thus it would not be correct to try to use this apologetic with one who is ready for an outright presentation of the gospel. At the same time, it could be very useful in either strengthening a believer's faith, or in presenting the claims of the gospel to a skeptical unbeliever.

# Part One

---

## A Resurrection Apologetic:
## Five Steps

# CHAPTER ONE

# Jesus' Resurrection as History

It has already been shown how the New Testament claims that the resurrection of Jesus is the center of the Christian faith and theology. For example, Paul asserts that various doctrines of Christianity are fallacious and ineffective if Jesus was not raised from the dead (I Cor. 15:12–19). In the Book of Acts we also find that the belief in a literal resurrection is the center of early Christian preaching (Acts 1:21, 22; 2:24, 32; etc.).

It is without much doubt that the resurrection is recognized by almost all theologians today as the central claim of the Christian faith, even by scholars who do not interpret this event literally. But, in spite of the widespread belief in the importance of this occurrence, the *literal* resurrection of Jesus has been assailed by critics since the Enlightenment.

An investigation into the truth of the resurrection has continued importance for Christians. Indeed, most agree that if this event were to be entirely abrogated, the entire Christian faith would be groundless.

On the other hand, if such a literal event was found to be

historically factual, then it would provide an even firmer basis for our faith. As a result, Christian theology would have a solid ground on which to build.

## An Investigation of the Resurrection

It is impossible to develop a complete apologetic for the resurrection within the scope of this chapter. Since I have done this in extended form in another work, however, a substantial background and various supportive arguments are thereby provided for the concise apologetic presented here.[1]

It should be mentioned at the outset that neither science nor history can rule out the literal resurrection (or other miracles) *a priori*. In other words, the facts must be investigated before a decision is made. This is true for two major reasons.

In the Enlightenment period, the universe was usually conceived of as a closed continuum of natural causes and effects. Since this view has been rejected by modern science, we can no longer postulate scientific or historical absolutes which are capable of ruling out events without an investigation. We therefore observe that since many unexpected and unpredictable events can and do occur, the modern outlook dictates that anything is possible and cannot be ruled out *a priori*.[2]

Second, we cannot rule out the resurrection *a priori*

---

[1]The author's work entitled *The Resurrection of Jesus: A Rational Inquiry*, was published in 1976 both as a book and in microfilm and is available from University Microfilms International, Ann Arbor, Michigan. As this book contains an extensive investigation of the historicity of the resurrection, such will not be reiterated here. However, repeated references will be made to this work in this first chapter so that the concise argument here will be more complete.

[2]For a more in-depth treatment see Gary Habermas, *The Resurrection of Jesus: A Rational Inquiry*, pp. 26-48.

because correct inductive research methods require that all possibilities be examined before a conclusion is drawn. Accordingly, lawyers, doctors, journalists, detectives and others must examine the facts before conclusions are made, whether it pertains to a lawsuit, curing a disease, interviewing eyewitnesses to correctly understand a news story, or finding a murderer.

Scientists likewise depend on the inductive method of examining all possibilities before a theory is postulated. This conclusion is corroborated by the accepted canon of scientific investigation which denies *a priori* rejections of data. As scientist James Long asserts:

> The hallmark of a scientist is that he has an open mind. He should not rule out *anything* without examining the probability of its occurring. Only after such an examination into the facts can a decision, based on probability, be made.[3]

Historians must also investigate the facts to ascertain if an event actually occurred. As stated by historian William Wand, there is no scholarly basis for rejecting data before such an investigation. Such *a priori* dismissals are not permissible, even if we do not like the conclusion arrived at by the facts. A critical scholar must base his decision on the evidence before him. For instance, if a miraculous event is the explanation best supported by the facts, it should be accepted as the most probable.[4]

Thus we see that conclusions drawn before (and even against) the facts are both non-scientific and non-historical. As we have briefly seen, the inductive method is utilized widely, by both science and history, as well as by other disciplines. We must also apply this principle to our

---

[3]Personal conversation with James Long (Ph.D., biochemistry), dated Feb. 10, 1977.
[4]See William Wand, *Christianity: A Historical Religion?* (Valley Forge: Judson Press, 1972), pp. 29-31, 51-52, 70-71.

historical study of the resurrection. In order to determine if this event literally occurred, we must investigate the facts to obtain the most probable conclusion which is based on the evidence. Such is the best means of arriving at valid historical data.[5]

We will now summarize the results of such an investigation of the facts concerning Jesus' resurrection. Using the inductive method as employed by historians, we will view primary sources, eyewitness testimony, archaeology, and critical responses to obtain the factual evidence.

### The Historical Facts

Theologians of various schools of thought differ as to the amount of historical fact they believe is to be found in the gospels. In spite of this, virtually all scholars agree that there are a number of facts surrounding the resurrection which are known to be historical.

It is accepted as a historical fact that Jesus died by Roman crucifixion and that He was buried.[6] It is also known that the disciples were bereaved and despondent as a result of His death. They were sure that His ministry had ended. We might add here that, although it is not as widely accepted as the other facts, an increasing number of critical theologians are beginning to acknowledge the historicity of the empty tomb.

It is agreed by almost all scholars that a few days after Jesus' death, the disciples and others had experiences in which they believed they actually saw the risen Jesus. History relates that the disciples underwent a radical transformation of their lives as a direct result of these experiences. They were transformed from timid and doubting

---

[5]See Ibid., pp. 49-59.
[6]The swoon theory of the nineteenth century has been largely abandoned in the twentieth century. Few, if any, reputable scholars doubt Jesus' death via crucifixion.

men into bold witnesses who proclaimed Jesus' resurrection even in the same city in which He had been crucified. It was from this testimony that the Christian church arose. Sunday (as opposed to Saturday, the Jewish Sabbath) became the chief day of worship. History also relates that an avowed enemy of Christianity and a persecutor of the church, Saul of Tarsus, was converted to Christianity by what he believed was an appearance of the resurrected Jesus.

This data reveals at least ten facts which are accepted as historical by virtually all scholars who study this subject, in spite of the various differences in other areas of their thought. (1) Jesus died because of crucifixion. (2) He was buried. (3) The disciples became very discouraged, having lost hope because of His death. (4) Jesus' tomb was found empty soon after His burial.[7] (5) A few days after Jesus' death, the disciples had experiences which they believed were literal appearances of the risen Jesus. (6) Because of these experiences, the disciples' lives were completely transformed to the point of being willing to die for their belief.

(7) The disciples' public testimony concerning the resurrection took place in Jerusalem, where Jesus was crucified and buried shortly before. (8) The Christian church had its beginning at this time. (9) Sunday became the primary day of worship. (10) A few years later, Paul became a believer because of an experience which he also believed to be an appearance of the risen Jesus.[8]

---

[7]In spite of the doubt of some scholars that the empty tomb was an original part of the resurrection message, it is included here because a number of recent studies in both Europe and America have confirmed its historicity. For an excellent summary of such studies, see Robert H. Stein's article "Was the Tomb Really Empty?", *Journal of the Evangelical Theological Society*, Vol. 20, No. 1, March (1977): pp. 23-29.

[8]Concerning these ten historical facts, cf. Habermas, *The Resurrection of Jesus: A Rational Inquiry*, pp. 314-316.

These ten facts are vital to our study of Jesus' resurrection. With the exception of the empty tomb, it is the virtually unanimous view of all theologians that these are the known historical facts. Therefore, any conclusions must properly account for them.

## Naturalistic Theories

The apologetic for the resurrection summarized here is based upon three major points. First, no proposed naturalistic theory attempting to explain the resurrection has yet properly accounted for all the accepted facts concerning this event. Naturalistic theories such as those alleging various types of fraud, a swoon, hallucinations (along with other psychological explanations), spiritualistic phenomena, and legends have all failed to disprove the resurrection. There are five reasons for dismissing these naturalistic theories.

The primary reason for the failure of these theories is that each of them has been disproven by several major objections, thus keeping them from being viable hypotheses.

It is not possible to detail how each of these theories has been refuted, but since I have shown this in much detail elsewhere,[9] one example should suffice to demonstrate the improbability of such naturalistic views.

One popular theory of the nineteenth century postulated that the disciples and other early believers experienced hallucinations and thereby believed that Jesus had risen. However, with the advent of twentieth-century psychology and psychiatry, and by using the historical facts

---

[9]See Ibid., pp. 114-171 for indepth refutations of the key naturalistic theories. In fact, a complete refutation of each theory was a major emphasis in this work, stressing that the more thorough such refutations are, the higher the probability for the resurrection becomes (cf. pp. 323-326). Although it is not, strictly speaking, a naturalistic theory, for a refutation of the more modern concept of the resurrection occurring in parahistory, see Ibid., pp. 198-224.

cited above, many substantial criticisms of this theory arise. First, hallucinations are subjective experiences in an individual's mind and therefore are not collective or contagious. Since these experiences cannot be shared or induced, the disciples could not all have had the same hallucination. Second, the psychological condition of the mind needed for hallucinations, characterized by belief and expectation, was lacking. The disciples were not expecting the resurrection but were in a state of despair. Third, the variety of times, places, and personalities involved in these experiences also militates against any hallucination theory. Fourth, care was taken to show that these experiences were not hallucinations. For instance, the New Testament clearly separates the resurrection appearances from subjective visions, thereby relating that Jesus' appearances were of a different quality. Fifth, hallucinations often stem from mental illness or from physiological sources such as deprivation of sleep and lack of food or drink. These conditions were not applicable to the disciples, however. Sixth, how do we explain the conversions of two non-believers, Paul and James? It is extremely doubtful that they would have desired to see Jesus enough to hallucinate.[10]

This provides just one instance of how the alternative theories have failed to account for the known facts concerning the resurrection. It also serves as an example of how each naturalistic hypothesis can be refuted by many objections.

Not one of these alternative views is capable of explaining all of the known historical facts by itself. The second reason for rejecting these naturalistic views is that to combine these theories is fruitless, simply because they were each found to be improbable. Therefore, based on the

---

[10]For a more complete refutation of the hallucination theory, see Habermas, Ibid., pp. 127-145.

individual failure of each of these naturalistic theories, it is even more difficult to refute the resurrection since a combination of improbable theories would only yield even more improbable results.

A third indication that the naturalistic theories have failed is that, generally speaking, liberals as a whole have used David Hume's essay "On Miracles"[11] as their major reason for rejecting the miraculous. However, Hume's essay against miracles fails noticeably in its attempt to rule out the miraculous. As I have critiqued this essay in much detail elsewhere,[12] a footnote should suffice to provide several key refutations.[13]

Thus we see that Hume's method of eliminating mira-

---

[11]Hume (1711-1776) theorized that miracles cannot be known to have occurred, since such events would be contrary to man's experience of the laws of nature, which dictates that miracles do not interrupt the normal course of events. To further back up his case, he argued from four supportive points, as well. (1) He held that there is no example of a miracle attested by witnesses who are incapable of presenting incorrect facts. (2) People enjoy gossiping about extraordinary events, even to the point of lying about them. (3) Miracles are usually claimed to occur among ignorant and barbarous peoples. (4) Miracles reported in the world religions cancel each other out. Hume's essay appeared as Section X of his work *An Enquiry Concerning Human Understanding*.

[12]See my chapter "Hume and Inerrancy" in the forthcoming book *Philosophical Roots of Biblical Errancy*, edited by Norman Geisler (Grand Rapids: Zondervan Publishing House, 1980). Cf. also Habermas, *The Resurrection of Jesus: A Rational Inquiry*, pp. 82-113.

[13]First, Hume commits several errors in logic, especially in his definition of miracles and his assumptions concerning man's experience in favor of and contrary to the miraculous. For instance, he defines these events so that it is impossible for them to occur from the outset. He even states that if *all* man's experience does not oppose a miracle, then it cannot even be called a miracle! He further asserts that no amount of evidence can establish a miracle. Such is anything but an unbiased look at the facts! Second, while speaking of the strength of the laws of nature, Hume ignores the possibility that God exists and that He may have set these laws aside temporarily in order to perform a miracle. But no amount of arguing from naturalistic premises inside a system can ever disprove the possibility that God has performed an event in nature from outside of it. Thus, as with all such naturalistic theories, the key question is not how strong nature is, but if God has broken into history by superseding these laws by a superior power. For instance, if the resurrection occurred, it would show that God did temporarily suspend nature's laws in order to perform this event (see Chapter II). Third, Hume additionally fails to accept a series of miracles (those of the eighteenth-century Jansenists) even though he admits that they were attested by excellent witnesses. He specifically rejects them not because of insufficient testimony but

cles is not valid. However, nineteenth-century liberal theologians used Hume's essay as the reasoning behind their rejection of miracles. For example, the well-known liberal scholar David Strauss concluded that Hume's essay conclusively disproved miracles and the question had been completely settled.[14] Other liberal scholars as a whole relied on Hume in their refusal to accept miracles.[15] As asserted by John Hermann Randall, Jr., because of Hume's essay, liberals rejected belief in miracles because such events were believed to interfere with the laws of nature.[16]

Despite the lack of philosophical and theological homogeneity especially in the last few decades, as represented by the various schools of thought, twentieth-century critical scholars have also rejected miracles based on Hume's argument.[17] It is thus plain that the influence of this philosopher's essay against miracles has extended until today.[18]

Because critical scholars since Hume have, as a whole,

---

because miraculous events are said not to occur. Fourth, Hume's four supportive points are historically invalid because if they were applied to history, very little (if anything!) could be known to have occurred. Yet we do not doubt the well-attested events of past history because they can be shown to be probable. This scholar was well aware of this and did not utilize these criteria in his own writing of history. Fifth, Hume's argument depends on the uniformity of nature when he denies this principle in his other works.

[14]David Friedrich Strauss, *A New Life of Jesus*, no translator given (Second edition; two volumes; London: Williams and Norgate, 1879), vol. I, p. 199.

[15]For primary-source treatments of Strauss, Schleiermacher, Paulus, Bruno Baur, Renan, Pfleiderer and von Harnack as examples of liberal theologians who rejected miracles due to Hume's argument, see Habermas, *The Resurrection of Jesus: A Rational Inquiry*, pp. 114–117, 151–152, 286–288.

[16]John Herman Randall, Jr., *The Making of the Modern Mind* (Revised edition; Boston: Houghton Mifflin Company, 1940), pp. 553–554.

[17]For primary-source treatments of the rejection of miracles via Hume's reasoning in theologians such as Tillich, Bultmann and John A. T. Robinson, see Habermas, *The Resurrection of Jesus: A Rational Inquiry*, pp. 117–118, 288–289. Analytical philosophers were also influenced very much by Hume in their rejection of miracles. See Chapter II, especially footnote 13.

[18]In addition to our above substantiation of this, see Randall, *The Making of the Modern Mind*, p. 293. Cf. Harvey Cox's testimony pertaining both to his own reliance on Hume's rejection of miracles and that of other contemporary

rejected miracles by using the arguments in his essay, and since they utilize reasons similar to those used by Hume as we just saw, they therefore employ erroneous notions. In other words, these arguments against miracles used by critical scholars since Hume are likewise invalid for reasons quite similar to those just raised against Hume. It is most imperative here that miracles not be ruled out because of the existence of the laws of nature and man's experience. Instead, we must ascertain whether there is a God who is stronger than these laws and who may choose to transcend them upon occasion.

The fourth reason for holding that naturalistic theories have failed to explain Jesus' resurrection is that even the nineteenth-century liberal theologians exposed the many inadequacies of these alternative theories themselves. For instance, Strauss exposed the flaws of the swoon theory which was popularized by Karl Venturini, Heinrich Paulus and others.[19] In fact, Strauss is believed by most scholars, both liberal and conservative, to have given the death blow to this theory.[20] By the turn of the twentieth century, both James Orr and Eduard Riggenbach remarked that this theory was no longer regarded by scholars as a viable explanation.[21]

On the other hand, Paulus and Schleiermacher pointed out various flaws in the hallucination theory held by Strauss, Renan, and others.[22] However, it was another liberal scholar, Theodor Keim, who presented the

---

scholars in "A Dialogue on Christ's Resurrection", *Christianity Today*, volume 12, number 14, 12 April 1968, pp. 5-12.

[19]Strauss, *A New Life of Jesus*, vol. I, pp. 408-412.

[20]For a liberal example, see Albert Schweitzer, *The Quest of the Historical Jesus*, translated by W. Montgomery (New York: The Macmillan Company, 1971), pp. 56-57.

[21]See James Orr, *The Resurrection of Jesus* (Grand Rapids: Zondervan Publishing House, 1908 edition reprinted in 1965), p. 92 and Eduard Riggenbach, *The Resurrection of Jesus* (New York: Eaton and Mains, 1907), pp. 48-49.

[22]See Friedrich Schleiermacher, *The Christian Faith*, edited by H. R. Mackintosh and J. S. Stewart (Two volumes; New York: Harper and Row, Publishers, 1963), vol. 2, p. 420; cf. Schweitzer, *The Quest of the Historical Jesus*, pp. 54-55.

strongest arguments against this subjective vision theory and is usually said to have disarmed this view.[23]

Later critical research on the resurrection, especially concerning the eyewitness testimony in the early Christian creed in I Cor. 15:3ff., disproved the legend theory which was popularized by the History of Religions school of thought.[24] Thus the legend theory was also judged to fall short of the known historical facts.

By these examples we can see how the nineteenth-century liberals themselves exposed the weaknesses and problems of each other's theories. In so doing they succeeded in demonstrating that none of these theories adequately accounted for the facts concerning the resurrection of Jesus.

The fifth and final indication that these naturalistic theories have failed is evident in the twentieth-century attitude towards them. While nineteenth-century critical scholars usually decimated each other's views individually, most critical scholars in this century have made a wholesale rejection of these views. An interesting feature in this recent rejection is that it is not confined to any one school of thought. Theologians of various persuasions have agreed in dismissing all of these naturalistic theories as untenable.

For instance, after listing the major naturalistic theories, neo-orthodox scholar Karl Barth states that such views have fallen into disfavor. One major problem with them is that they are inconsistent with the facts. Thus, Barth explains that these theories are no longer considered by scholars.[25]

---

[23]For example, see Orr, *The Resurrection of Jesus,* p. 219.

[24]See Reginald Fuller *The Formation of the Resurrection Narratives* (New York: The Macmillan Company, 1971), pp. 9–14, 48; cf. especially Wolfhart Pannenberg, *Jesus—God and Man,* translated by Lewis L. Wilkens and Duane Priebe (Philadelphia: The Westminster Press, 1968), pp. 90–91.

[25]Karl Barth, *Church Dogmatics,* edited by G. W. Bromiley and T. F. Torrence (13 volumes; Edinburgh: T. and T. Clark, 1961), Volume IV, Part One, p. 340.

In a similar vein, eminent Roman Catholic theologian Raymond E. Brown gives a list of nineteenth-century theories. Brown asserts not only that these views are not held today, but that they are no longer even respectable. Furthermore, he states that any new revivals of such views should be ignored by serious scholars.[26]

Similar instances could be taken from the works of critical scholars in other schools of thought, such as Paul Tillich, Wolfhart Pannenberg and Günther Bornkamm, all of whom have shown the futility of these alternative theories.[27] Suffice it to say that since even the critical theologians are pointing out errors and dismissing these theories (like conservative scholars have often done), this is a further indication of the failure of these alternative theories.

To summarize briefly, the first point of our two point apologetic for Jesus' resurrection concerns the failure of naturalistic theories which have been proposed to account for this event. We saw that these alternative theories failed for five key reasons. First, we found that each theory is opposed by several major objections which serve to refute it and thus nullify it as a viable hypothesis.

Second, we found that no naturalistic theory can explain all of the known historical facts by itself. Therefore we need a combination of improbable theories, which only leads to compounded improbability. Third, liberals from Schleiermacher to the present have followed Hume's reasoning in their rejection of miracles. Therefore, their attempts to dismiss the miraculous are invalid for reasons very similar to those raised against Hume. Once again, in

---

[26]Raymond E. Brown, "The Resurrection and Biblical Criticism" in *Commonweal*, Nov. 24 (1967): p. 233.
[27]Cf. Paul Tillich, *Systematic Theology* (Three Volumes; Chicago: The University of Chicago Press, 1951, 1957, 1963), Volume II, pp. 153-158; Pannenberg, *Jesus—God and Man*, pp. 88-106; Günther Bornkamm, *Jesus of Nazareth*, translated by Irene and Fraser McLuskey with James M. Robinson (New York: Harper and Row, Publishers, 1960), pp. 180-186.

order to perceive if a miracle has occurred, we must ascertain if there is a God who has acted in history by temporarily suspending the laws of nature (see Chapter 2).

Fourth, the nineteenth-century liberal scholars decimated each other's theories, thereby pointing out the inherent weaknesses in each view. Fifth, twentieth-century critical thought has rejected these naturalistic theories as a whole in relating that such are seldom held by critical scholars today.

Based on this inductive evidence we can conclude that such naturalistic theories are not able to account for Jesus' resurrection. Thus this literal event remains unrefuted by such attempts.

## Evidences for Jesus' Resurrection

The second major reason for postulating that the resurrection of Jesus literally occurred in history is that there are at least ten positive, corroborating evidences for this event, which we will only be able to briefly explain here. Therefore, not only is there the fact that no naturalistic theory has been able to explain the resurrection, but there are also a number of other evidences supporting the literal event which give it the status of probability.

It should be mentioned at the outset that these evidences are taken from the list of accepted facts which was provided above. In other words, the evidences being presented here are agreed to by virtually all scholars (even of differing schools of thought) as historical facts. The most obvious advantage of this is that these evidences would themselves be seen as historical and therefore would not be rejected as having no historical basis. Because of this acceptance, each of these historical evidences would logically have to be explained away in order for the resurrection to be rejected as a historical event itself.

The first evidence is the empirical experiences which the

disciples claimed concerning their having witnessed appearances of the risen Jesus. This is the most important evidence both because there are no valid naturalistic theories to explain these appearances and because there are additional positive reasons for accepting them, as we will now perceive.

Second, the change in the disciples from normal men concerned only with their own welfare into bold preachers who were even willing to die for their faith effectively demonstrates that they believed that they had seen Jesus. That these men were totally convinced of this fact is also admitted by critical scholars.[28] But how do we explain this belief apart from Jesus' literal resurrection, especially when naturalistic theories have failed?

The third evidence in favor of this event is the inability of the Jewish leaders to disprove it in the very city in which Jesus died and was buried. Of all the enemies of Christ's message, these men were in the best position to expose any error, both because of their opposition to this teaching and because of their location in the exact area in which the evidence could best be checked. This is a key evidence in favor of Jesus' resurrection because the Jewish leaders were the skeptics and yet even they could not refute the evidence.

Fourth, the resurrection was the center of the earliest Christian preaching. This is a fact admitted by essentially all scholars, based especially on Paul's use of the ancient creed in I Cor. 15:3ff., as we saw above. This creed probably dates from the 30s A.D., as it notes that the disciples'

---

[28]For a sampling, see Bultmann's essay "New Testament and Mythology" in *Kerygma and Myth,* edited by Hans Werner Bartsch (New York: Harper and Row, Publishers, 1961), p. 42; see also Tillich, *Systematic Theology,* vol. 2, p. 154. For a statement as to the acceptance of this fact by critical scholars as a whole, see the article "Jesus Christ" by S. MacLean Gilmour and William P. Patterson in *Dictionary of the Bible,* edited by James Hastings, revised edition by Frederick C. Grant and H. H. Rowley (New York: Charles Scribner's Sons, 1963), p. 490.

experiences immediately followed Jesus' crucifixion, beginning only three days later. This early creed thus demonstrates that the resurrection was not derived from ancient myths and legends, since this report follows directly after Jesus' crucifixion (about 30 A.D.).[29]

That legends cannot account for the origin of this earliest proclamation is further indicated by the fact that it was the disciples who both participated in these occurrences (I Cor. 15:5-8) and who testified about their own experiences (verses 11-14). Thus the proclamation of Jesus' resurrection extends back to the original eyewitnesses and not to myths or legends which were added later. In other words, the origin of the disciples' message concerning the resurrected Christ lies in their actual eyewitness experiences and not ancient myths.[30] Since these experiences are not refuted by alternative theories, they provide strong evidence for Jesus' resurrection.

The evidence for the empty tomb constitutes a fifth evidence for Jesus' rising from the dead. In recent years, an increasing number of critical theologians such as Reginald Fuller, John A. T. Robinson and Wolfhart Pannenberg have recognized the evidence for the empty tomb and even the historicity of it.[31] To be sure, an empty tomb does not guarantee a resurrection, but it does serve as a pointer to such an event. And if a literal resurrection is denied,

---

[29]See Fuller, *The Formation of the Resurrection Narratives,* pp. 9-14, 48; Pannenberg, *Jesus—God and Man,* pp. 90-91; cf. Habermas, *The Resurrection of Jesus: A Rational Inquiry,* pp. 154-156.
[30]This provides a somewhat more complete explanation of I Cor. 15:3ff. and its ramifications, which were briefly mentioned earlier. See also Habermas, *The Resurrection of Jesus: A Rational Inquiry,* pp. 146-171.
[31]Fuller, *The Formation of the Resurrection Narratives,* pp. 48-49, 69-70, 179-180; Pannenberg, *Jesus—God and Man,* pp. 100-104. Robinson's less enthusiastic but nonetheless positive treatment of the empty tomb is found, for instance, in his work *Exploration into God* (Stanford: Stanford University Press, 1967), p. 113. In spite of this, we still realize that the empty tomb is not as well accepted as the other facts, which are accepted by almost all scholars, as we saw earlier.

then an additional naturalistic theory is needed to account for the empty tomb.

The very existence of the Christian church is a sixth evidence for the resurrection, especially when we recall that this institution was founded on the resurrection. The church would never have had a beginning if the Savior upon whose teachings it was built was dead, not even being able to conquer death himself. Without this event there would have been no Pentecost. But how else can we explain the existence of the church?

A seventh and somewhat related evidence is the use of Sunday as the Christian day of worship ever since the time of the early church. We too often forget that the first Christians were monotheistic Jews, accustomed to worshiping on Saturday. Yet we find Christians utilizing Sunday as their special day (cf. Acts 20:7; I Cor. 16:1-2). It is plain that Sunday is the commemoration of the day on which Jesus rose (Luke 24:1; Matt. 28:1; Rev. 1:10). But how can we account for this observance apart from Jesus' resurrection appearances on the first Easter Sunday?

The conversion of Saul of Tarsus, probably the best known persecutor of Christians, provides an eighth strong evidence of the reality of Jesus' rising from the dead. That Paul was converted to Christianity is denied by no one. Yet such a drastic change surely demands a good explanation. Paul had no doubt that he had met the risen Jesus (I Cor. 9:1; etc.). Is there a more probable cause which really explains what occurred to him?

The ninth evidence concerns another conversion of an unbeliever. That James, the brother of Jesus, was opposed to Christian teachings before the resurrection is well recognized (see John 7:5; cf. Mark 3:21).[32] That he was a

---

[32]Raymond E. Brown, *The Virginal Conception and Bodily Resurrection of Jesus* (New York: Paulist Press, 1973) p. 94, footnote 160.

leader of the Jerusalem church later is equally established (see Acts 15; Gal. 1:18-19 for example). Paul reports that a key intervening event was an appearance to James by the resurrected Jesus (I Cor. 15:7). How else do we account for his conversion, which was so radically contrary to his former beliefs, especially when we recall that family members would often be the hardest to convince on such matters?

The conversion of James is so noteworthy that even from a critical viewpoint, Reginald Fuller concludes that if Paul had not recorded this appearance to James, we would still have to accept such an appearance in order to account for both James' post-resurrection conversion and the subsequent speed with which he acquired a position of leadership in the early church![33] Such a conclusion provides a valuable insight into this important issue.

The tenth and final evidence is not one of the ten accepted historical facts, yet it builds on the others. It is, however, a corroboration of the resurrection. This is the evidence supplied by Jesus' own predictions of His resurrection. Although these are often denied by critics, this is obviously because they also deny the literal event. But I would hold that it is fruitless to object to these predictions if the actual raising of Jesus is already probable, based on the other evidences. The special value of these predictions is that they show that the resurrection was not simply a coincidence, or a "freak event," but rather a performance of God of which Jesus had foreknowledge.[34]

How can we explain all of these ten evidences apart from Jesus' literal resurrection *and* postulate a probable naturalistic theory against this event when none were found to be plausible? Yet this is what would have to be

---

[33]Fuller, Ibid., p. 37.
[34]We will return both to a defense of the validity of these predictions and to their importance in the next chapter.

done in order to explain away the resurrection. In particular, when the eyewitness experiences of the disciples, James, and Paul are considered along with their corresponding transformations, the literal resurrection is shown to be the best explanation for the facts. This is especially so in light of the failure of the naturalistic theories to account for the historical facts.

## An Additional Apologetic

A third extremely strong evidential point in favor of the historicity of Jesus' resurrection concerns a further usage of the ten accepted historical facts surrounding this event which were given at the beginning of this chapter. It is this author's belief that even if we were to use only four of these facts,[35] we would still have a sufficient case by which we could demonstrate that this event is probable.[36]

The four facts we will utilize here are: Jesus' death by crucifixion, the disciples' experiences which they believed to be appearances of the risen Jesus, the subsequent transformation of these men, and the conversion of Saul of Tarsus because of an experience which he also believed was an appearance of the risen Jesus. These four "core historical facts" are unanimously accepted as historical by virtually all scholars who study this subject, in spite of differences in other areas of their thought.[37] These four

---

[35] It is important to note that these ten facts (and, ultimately the four "core facts") are not accepted in this work simply because they are admitted by essentially all scholars who deal with this subject. Rather, and even more importantly, they are accepted here because the historical evidence reveals that they are probable historical facts.

[36] It should also be noted that we are choosing these four facts so as to make our case for Jesus' resurrection more convincing and not because the other six facts are not as well accepted by scholars.

[37] For a sampling of the critical scholars who accept these four "core historical facts" see, Fuller, *The Formation of the Resurrection Narratives*, especially pp. 27–49;

facts are capable, on a smaller scale, both of disproving the naturalistic theories and of providing key positive evidences for the resurrection, as an example will now illustrate.

The facts surrounding and supporting Jesus' death disprove the swoon theory. The disciples' experiences rule out the hallucination theory and other subjective theories both because such phenomena are not contagious, being witnessed by one person alone and because of the variety of time and place factors involved, as already noted above. That it was the disciples who had these experiences also rules out the legend or myth theory because the original teaching of the resurrection is thus based on real eyewitness experiences and not on later legends. The disciples' transformation shows that they really believed that Jesus rose from the dead and disproves the fraud (stolen body) theory both because of this change and because liars do not make martyrs. Paul's conversion also points out the futility of the hallucination and most other theories because Paul was an avid enemy and persecutor of the church and was not in the proper frame of mind for hallucinations, nor would he be convinced by lies. In addition, the fact that Paul also had a real experience similarly rules out the swoon and legend theories.[38]

---

Bultmann, "New Testament and Mythology", especially pp. 34-42; Bultmann, *Theology of the New Testament*, translated by Kendrick Grobel (Two volumes; New York: Charles Scribner's Sons, 1951, 1955), volume I, pp. 44-45; Tillich, *Systematic Theology*, volume II, pp. 153-158; Bornkamm, *Jesus of Nazareth*, pp. 179-186; Jürgen Moltmann, *Theology of Hope*, translated by James W. Leitch (New York: Harper and Row, Publishers, 1967), especially pp. 197-202; Pannenberg, *Jesus—God and Man*, pp. 88-106; Paul Van Buren, *The Secular Meaning of the Gospel* (New York: The Macmillan Company, 1963), pp. 126-134; Raymond E. Brown, *The Virginal Conception and Bodily Resurrection of Jesus*, especially pp. 81-92.

[38]The other six facts provide even more complete refutations of these theories, such as the disciples' despair and disillusionment showing that they were not in the proper frame of mind for hallucinations and the resurrection being the center of the earliest Christian teaching (as in the creed in I Cor. 15:3ff.) showing that this teaching immediately followed the event and was not due to legends.

This is only an example of how these four core historical facts are capable of ruling out the naturalistic theories.

These core facts also provide positive evidences for the resurrection, such as the appearances which cannot be explained away naturalistically, the transformation of the disciples, who were willing to die for their faith, and the conversion of Paul, a skeptic and persecutor of the church, causing him to be transformed to the point of dying for his faith as well. These evidences, in particular, are able to show that the resurrection is the best explanation for the known facts.

The importance of this additional apologetic cannot be overestimated, as it has other important functions besides what we have just seen. Since these four facts are established by critical and historical procedures, contemporary theologians cannot reject our evidence for the resurrection simply by rejecting the inspiration of the Scriptures (or other criteria), as we will now see. A few examples will readily show the further use of these four facts.

It is also impossible to rule out the resurrection merely by citing scriptural "discrepancies." Not only can such claims be refuted, but, as we have just shown, the resurrection can be demonstrated as probable even when the minimum amount of known historical facts are utilized. Thus, although some may have doubts concerning the Scriptural texts[39] on other issues, these four core historical facts which scholars know to be reliable history are sufficient in themselves to demonstrate the resurrection.

For this same reason, one cannot simply say, as is popular today, that "something happened to the disciples, but we do not know what it was" due to such reasons as the

---

[39]Later we will address ourselves to the question of the reliability and inspiration of Scripture.

subjective quality of writing history or because of the "cloudiness" of the New Testament texts. Likewise, the contemporary popularity of a "spiritual resurrection" whereby Jesus is risen in the present preaching of the church, but not literally, is also in error.[40] Once again, we must reject such views because the facts which are admitted by all scholars as knowable history are adequate to demonstrate the literal resurrection. Therefore, although we do not know everything that happened to the disciples, we do know enough to conclude according to probability that Jesus rose from the dead and appeared literally to the original eyewitnesses.[41]

## Conclusion

We must conclude our investigation with the decision that the resurrection of Jesus is a highly probable historical fact. Our study has been brief, but it has dealt with many key issues. We saw that it is easier to accept this literal event than it is to refute this threefold apologetic by offering a probable set of naturalistic theories which adequately account for all of the facts *and* by explaining away these ten evidences.

A major thrust of this chapter has been to argue that the claims of the earliest eyewitnesses have thereby been vindicated,[42] since the evidence does indicate that Jesus' resurrection is a literal historical event. Building on the accepted historical facts, this conclusion is based on both the failure of the naturalistic theories on one hand and the

---

[40]See Habermas, *The Resurrection of Jesus: A Rational Inquiry,* pp. 293-298 for further refutations of such positions.

[41]See Ibid., pp. 314-316, 322.

[42]While no judgment was made as to the exact composition of Jesus' resurrection body, the evidence does reveal that He rose in a change (or spiritual) body, as perceived by the eyewitnesses (see Appendix 3).

existence of several positive evidences for these appearances on the other. When combined, these show that Jesus' appearances are the best explanation for the facts. This apologetic was additionally supported in that the known historical facts which are accepted by critics (and the "core" facts, in particular) are enough to verify the probability of the resurrection. The critic's doubts on other issues thus do not change this basic conclusion. As a result, contemporary scholars should accept the historicity of this event, since it can be demonstrated according to critical and historical procedures. Therefore, the literal resurrection of Jesus is a probable historical event, as the best explanation of the historical facts.

Based on this conclusion of the factualness of the resurrection, we will now turn to the question of Christian theology. It will be our contention that the resurrection serves as a firm basis for theology. We will illustrate the first point of our apologetic as follows:

## STEP 1

JESUS' RESURRECTION

1. **No viable naturalistic theories.**

2. **Ten positive evidences.**

3. **Accepted and "core" historical facts.**

# CHAPTER TWO

# The Existence of God

We have concluded thus far that the resurrection of Jesus is a literal historical event. In this chapter we will endeavor to ascertain if there are rational connections between this event and the existence of God. However, some philosophers have judged that *God-talk* is meaningless. Thus, before we can deal with the relationship between the resurrection and God's existence, we must first ascertain if it is even possible to talk about God.

## Logical Positivism and Linguistic Analysis

Logical positivism and·linguistic analysis have three major geographical roots. First, Scottish philosopher David Hume held several views which influenced these twentieth-century schools of thought. Hume's rejection of miracles has provided the major impetus for rejecting the miraculous.[1] Hume's doubts concerning God's existence

---

[1] *An Enquiry Concerning Human Understanding*, Section X.

have also carried weight,[2] as has his intriguing statement in his *An Enquiry Concerning Human Understanding* whereby he casts doubt on statements which are neither true by definition nor true by empirical investigation.[3]

Second, French philosopher Auguste Comte's (1798–1857) brand of positivism arises chiefly from his threefold classification of the stages of thought through which man has passed. In ancient times, man is said to have employed *theological* reasoning, using God as an answer to life's questions. Next, man utilized *metaphysical,* or abstract, reasoning without the proper factual basis. But modern man emphasizes *positive* reasoning, which is a reliance on the scientific method.[4]

Third, Austria was an important center in the formation of logical positivism. Ludwig Wittgenstein (1889–1951) came from this country and later taught philosophy at Cambridge. He stressed the proper usage of language and its importance in philosophy.[5] In the 1920s, Moritz Schlick (1882–1936) formed and led the Vienna Circle, a group of philosophers strongly influenced by Wittgenstein's language analysis.

A. J. Ayer popularized the teachings of logical positivism with the appearance of his work *Language, Truth and Logic* in 1936. This book familiarized many with the "verification principle." Briefly, it taught that meaningful statements are either analytical and therefore true by definition (such as with pure logic, mathematics, or other tautological statements) or synthetic, meaning that they can be validated by empirical investigation (based upon probabilities arising from sense experience). If statements fall into neither of these categories, then they are said to be factu-

---

[2]See *Dialogues Concerning Natural Religion.*
[3]Section XII, Part III.
[4]Comte's chief work is his *Course of Positive Philosophy.*
[5]Wittgenstein's opus is his *Tractatus Logico—Philosophicus.*

ally meaningless because they are incapable of empirical verification.[6]

Early positivists, judging by these criteria, usually concluded that theological and ethical statements were factually meaningless (although sometimes granting them emotive significance) because they could not be verified. However, in the last few decades philosophers have turned from logical positivism to a less rigid application of such rules. In this and other respects linguistic analysis is generally considered to be a modified outgrowth of logical positivism. More attention has been given to language analysis,[7] such as the principle of falsification in language (i.e., under what conditions would a certain statement be invalid?).[8] However, some of the most recent trends indicate that theology is no longer judged by strict verificational procedures.

It should be noted here that by no means are all linguistic analysts opposed to *God-talk* or even to verification of certain principles of theism. Beliefs such as God's existence, miracles, and immortality are at least discussed in a congenial way and are sometimes defended.[9] Thus, far from speaking with a unanimous voice, analytic philosophers are divided over the question of whether such principles of theology are verifiable.

This leads us to a critique of logical positivism and lin-

---

[6]See A. J. Ayer, *Language, Truth and Logic* (New York: Dover Publications, 1946), p. 5, for instance.

[7]Cf. Van Buren, *The Secular Meaning of the Gospel,* pp. 14-15. We will deal below with the major philosophical reason as to why the verification principle became used less rigidly.

[8]See especially Anthony Flew, "Theology and Falsification" in *New Essays in Philosophical Theology,* edited by Anthony Flew and Aladair MacIntyre (New York: The Macmillan Company, 1955). This essay is also included in John Hick's (editor) *The Existence of God* (New York: The Macmillan Company, 1964), pp. 225-228.

[9]For an excellent example of such responses by a number of leading linguistic analysts, see John Donnelly, editor *Logical Analysis and Contemporary Theism* (New York: Fordham University Press, 1972).

guistic analysis. It must be remembered here, however, that not all the philosophers of these persuasions reject *God-talk* and the supernatural. Nonetheless, four substantial critiques will be briefly raised against those who reject God and His possible intervention into human history.

First, logical positivism suffered several philosophical setbacks, the major problem being that the verification principle itself could not be verified, thus meaning that it did not stand up to its own test. It was obvious that the verification principle was not valid by definition because, for example, it is not proper to rule out another's view simply by defining your position to be correct. But it was equally obvious that no empirical verification could prove that empirical results were the only valid way of gaining knowledge. Thus, positivism had failed to abide by its own epistemological criteria. It could not invalidate theology simply because, in trying to do so, it invalidated itself.

Even Ayer realized that the verification principle was faulty in this regard and thus he later allowed for the possibility of meaningfulness for metaphysical claims. In fact, he even pointed out that metaphysical statements could not be eliminated apart from an investigation of particular arguments.[10] This opens the way to an examination of the Christian theist's arguments and showed that the verification principle was not a valid guide for eliminating such theistic claims especially when the evidence indicates otherwise. Therefore, due to this first criticism and other similar ones, logical positivism is no longer considered to be a viable option in philosophy today.[11]

---

[10] See Ayer, *Language, Truth and Logic,* Introduction (written in 1946), pp. 5-26, especially pp. 15-16.
[11] For a succinct summary of some of these philosophical problems with logical positivism, see David Elton Trueblood, *Philosophy of Religion* (Grand Rapids: Baker Book House, 1973), pp. 195-202.

Second, several linguistic analysts still follow Hume's essay against miracles in order to rule out such events.[12] As noted above, those who rely on Hume for their rejection of miracles fall prey to virtually the same criticisms as did Hume. In particular, we must remember that no naturalistic arguments which view the strength of the laws of nature from within the system can ever dictate as to whether the system itself was temporarily interrupted by the superior power of God's working in history from the outside. It is therefore necessary to ascertain if evidence exists for God's existence and for such a temporary suspension of nature's law by a superior power.[13]

Third, to oppose the resurrection at all (as the chief example of a miracle-claim) would still involve formulating a probable naturalistic theory as to *why* it did not occur. Merely to refer to linguistic analysis, for instance, offers no theory to account for the facts.[14] Utilizing the falsification

---

[12]See Richard Swineburne, *The Concept of Miracle* (New York: The Macmillan Company and St. Martin's Press, 1970), pp. 18-21 and R. F. Holland's essay "The Miraculous" in Donnelly, *Logical Analysis and Contemporary Theism*, pp. 218-235 for discussions of such views which are dependent on Hume (or an expansion of his thought.)

[13]See Gary Habermas, "Hume and Inerrancy" in the forthcoming book *Philosophical Roots of Biblical Errancy*, edited by Norman Geisler (Grand Rapids: Zondervan Publishing House, 1980). To summarize briefly, updating Hume's essay also falls prey to many of the same criticisms as we applied to Hume himself. For instance, one cannot arbitrarily mount evidence against a miracle assuming that one could never happen, nor is it logical to define miracles so that they don't occur, such as by expanding nature to include miracles as natural events. Additionally, a critical investigation is still needed to ascertain if God exists and if He did temporarily suspend the laws of nature, as we just noted. Even the repeatability of scientific laws cannot answer whether God simply suspended the laws by a superior power. Only research can determine such action. Lastly, as will be pointed out later in this chapter, there are certain indications that events such as Jesus' resurrection cannot be accounted for at all by the laws of nature. Rather, this event requires that God did indeed suspend the laws of nature by a superior power.

[14]The linguistic analyst who has probably directed the most attention to Jesus' resurrection from a negative viewpoint is Paul Van Buren. This critical scholar also admits that the disciples had some kind of experience of Jesus, that "something" happened, but he does not count it as a historical resurrection (*The Secular*

principle we can assert that if any of the major naturalistic theories could entirely explain away this event, then the resurrection of Jesus would be shown to be false. But to formulate such an alternative theory is quite improbable since each is opposed by several objections and none are able to account for the facts surrounding the resurrection.

Fourth, positivists and linguistic analysts accept history as a valid means of ascertaining empirical truth.[15] Therefore, our positive decision in favor of the historicity of Jesus' resurrection is actually a positive decision in favor of an empirical event of the past, based on the empirical experiences of the earliest eyewitnesses. In other words, Jesus' resurrection is an empirically demonstrable event, as we found in our study above.

To summarize briefly, we see that naturalistic positivism and linguistic analysis fail for at least four reasons. The verification principle itself could not be verified, therefore meaning that it could not be used to refer to theology as meaningless. Next, such scholars are in error in following Hume, especially in not investigating history to ascertain if there is evidence of God's performing a miracle by temporarily suspending nature's laws by a power superior to that of the laws of nature. Also, to oppose the resurrection involves the use of naturalistic theories when none were found to be probable. Lastly, the resurrection can be his-

---

*Meaning of the Gospel,* pp. 126-134). Van Buren's treatment fails for at least two general reasons. First, his view teaches some type of subjective experience and thus falls prey to virtually all the various criticisms which were given above of the hallucination theory (for a more complete and specific refutation of such subjective experiences, see Habermas, *The Resurrection of Jesus: A Rational Inquiry,* pp. 144-145, footnote 104). Second, Van Buren admits all of the four core historical facts (*The Secular Meaning of the Gospel,* pp. 126-134), which, as we saw, are capable of demonstrating the historicity of the literal resurrection by themselves, independently of other doubts.

[15]For a few examples, see Ayer, *Language, Truth and Logic,* especially p. 19 in the Introduction to the 1946 edition; cf. p. 40 in the 1936 edition; Swinburne, *The Concept of Miracle,* pp. 33-51; Van Buren, Ibid., pp. 126, 128, 129, 167.

torically validated as an empirical event and thus must be accepted as historical, as we found in Chapter 1.

Now we perceive that linguistic analysis can actually be an ally of Christian theology for at least two reasons.[16] First, it shows that irrational theologies which take leaps of faith cannot be either verified or falsified, which gives them a questionable epistemological value.

Second, it shows that Christian theology is on firm grounds in that it is empirically verifiable through the resurrection of Jesus. Christian theology is by no means nonsense or meaningless, since it is built on a space-time, empirical event.

In answer to our original question, we must now conclude that it is quite possible to talk about God's existence. Logical positivism cannot annul this conclusion, because in so doing it disqualifies itself, as already noted. In addition, we can speak of the historicity of the resurrection as an empirical event. The way is also left open to other rational evidences for God's existence, such as theistic proofs. At any rate, we may turn now to the relationship between Jesus' resurrection and God's existence, having verified the former and established a grounds for discussing the latter.

## Theistic Arguments

One final and significant critique of logical positivism and linguistic analysis is that there are viable theistic arguments which reveal that God does indeed exist. This is also an extremely important conclusion in terms of our

---

[16]We cannot claim logical positivism as an ally, since we already saw that it was invalid on its own grounds and no longer formally exists as a philosophical school of thought.

study, since if God is shown to exist on other grounds apart from the resurrection, such as by theistic argumentation, then it may be possible to ascertain that raising Jesus was an act in accordance with His attributes. By these means it may be possible to require even less direct evidence to affirm God's intervention in this historical occurrence, since it would actually be expected in terms of what these arguments reveal concerning the Person of God.[17]

There are four classical arguments for God's existence. The cosmological argument begins with the finite world or some aspect of it and argues for the need of an infinite cause for this world. The teleological argument progresses from the design in the universe to a designer of the universe. The ontological argument asserts that the idea of an infinite, necessary and perfect Being demands that such a Being exists, since a necessary Being must necessarily exist. The moral argument has also gained much in popularity and importance since Immanuel Kant. It argues from an objective moral law in the universe and in man's heart and mind to the existence of a moral lawgiver.

Because we cannot deal with each of these arguments separately in the scope of this work,[18] we will limit this discussion to a brief exposition of three strong forms of theistic argumentation.

## Human Reason and the Existence of God

The first argument is proposed by C. S. Lewis in his work *Miracles.*[19] In a chapter entitled "The Self-Contradiction of the Naturalist," Lewis points out that all knowl-

---

[17]Swinburne, *The Concept of Miracle,* pp. 65–71.
[18]For an excellent survey of these arguments, see Norman Geisler, *Philosophy of Religion* (Grand Rapids: Zondervan Publishing House, 1974), pp. 87–189.
[19]C. S. Lewis, *Miracles: A Preliminary Study* (New York: The Macmillan Company, 1947).

edge depends on the validity of man's reasoning process. Unless human reason is valid, no science can be said to be true and, even further, we could never know whether any proposition is true or false. Since all knowledge relies on the validity of rational thought, it may be stated "as a rule that *no thought is valid if it can be fully explained as the result of irrational causes.*"[20]

Thus, human reason as a whole is valueless if it comes about, and can be accounted for, irrationally. It follows from this that any philosophical world view which postulates that the human mind is a result of irrational causes is unacceptable, for there could be no such thing as knowledge. But naturalism holds that the mind developed by chance, as opposed to rational beginnings through God's creation.

However, if we simply came to exist through chance and our thinking is simply a motion of atoms, we have no reason to believe that we think rationally or even that we can think at all. Any argument to disprove this position must assume the very point which it is endeavoring to disprove, namely, the reality of rational thought.

In other words, the universe may be one big irrational machine. What appears to be rational could be irrational if we come from irrational causes. How can we know? In fact, this is the real crux of the issue because we cannot *know* anything if we exist and think by chance. It simply must be *assumed* that we can know in such a world view.

If the naturalist takes a pragmatic view such as doing what works, it must be pointed out that this is a retreat from the original thesis that naturalism is the correct world view. If naturalism cannot be known to be true, it leaves the question open as to which world view is correct.[21]

---

[20]Ibid., pp. 19-21.
[21]Ibid., pp. 21-24.

To repeat, it was found that irrational beginnings cannot produce rational thought (at least that which we can *know* is rational). Therefore, if rational thought cannot come from an irrational world view, yet rational thought still exists, then it must proceed from a rational mind. The alternative is to deny rational thought altogether. Again, any argument to disprove this position *assumes* that this rationale is also valid.[22]

Admittedly, Lewis' argument does not present an absolute case for theism in that it might also be concluded here that the universe is irrational. Yet this is still a formidable argument, since few would care to deny the validity of rational thought, which would lead, in all probability, to Lewis' final conclusion. In other words, rational thinking is evidence of God's existence.

### Existential Causality

We will now turn to a second (and stronger) argument of the cosmological variety. Two very important versions of this argument are those of Thomas Aquinas, which is based on existential causality, and Gottfried Leibniz, which relies on the principle of sufficient reason.[23] Because of Thomas's existential basis in reality, his argument is stronger than that of Leibniz, which demands only an explanation in the area of reason.[24]

To give an example of how such a cosmological argument from existential causality operates,[25] Geisler gives the following summary:

---

[22]Ibid., pp. 25-29.

[23]Others like Moses Maimonides and Duns Scotus utilized arguments like Thomas', while Christian Wolff is probably the best known supporter of the Leibnizian argument.

[24]For substantiation of this, see Geisler, *Philosophy of Religion*, pp. 180-181, 190-226. Thomas' argument is found, for instance, in his *Summa Theologica*, Part One, Questions II, III.

[25]Others have also defended similar formulations of this argument. See Bruce

(1) Some things undeniably exist (e.g., I cannot deny my own existence).

(2) My nonexistence is possible.

(3) Whatever has the possibility not to exist is currently caused to exist by another.

(4) There cannot be an infinite regress of current causes of existence.

(5) Therefore, a first uncaused cause of my current existence exists.

(6) This uncaused cause must be infinite, unchanging, all-powerful, all-knowing, and all-perfect.

(7) This infinitely perfect being is appropriately called "God."

(8) Therefore, God exists.

(9) This God who exists is identical to the God described in the Christian Scriptures.

(10) Therefore, the God described in the Bible exists.[26]

We cannot reproduce the subsequent explication of each point and the answering of objections which follows due to the length of the apologetic.[27] Suffice it to say, however, that Geisler presents a very strong case for the existence of God based on the principle of existential causality. Indeed, Geisler claims undeniability on behalf of this argument. He concludes his defense with this assertion: "In brief, if any finite being exists, then an infinite being exists as an actual and necessary ground for finite being."[28]

---

Reichenbach, *The Cosmological Argument: A Reassessment* (Springfield: Charles C. Thomas, 1972) and William Rowe, *The Cosmological Argument* (Princeton: Princeton University Press, 1975).

[26]Norman Geisler, *Christian Apologetics* (Grand Rapids: Baker Book House, 1976), pp. 238–239.

[27]See Ibid., pp. 239–250 and Geisler, *Philosophy of Religion*, pp. 190–226 for a defense of these assertions and answers to criticisms of the cosmological argument.

[28]Geisler, *Philosophy of Religion*, p. 224.

## The Second Law of Thermodynamics

Our third theistic argument is another variety of the cosmological argument for God's existence and has gained popularity mainly from a scientific standpoint. This approach is based on the Second Law of Thermodynamics, a well established scientific law. It seems that this scientific cosmological argument can complement the philosophical argument just provided.

Simply stated, the Second Law of Thermodynamics asserts that energy in the universe is becoming less and less available for use because all natural processes are moving irreversibly towards greater entropy or randomness. This means, therefore, that the universe is running down to the point of an eventual heat death.

The cosmological implications of this Second Law are great. For instance, we find that the universe is not eternal. It must have had a beginning at a point in time, as indicated by its running down. Thus, if it had a beginning, a beginner is needed to explain its origin.[29]

According to philosopher Elton Trueblood, it can now be said in light of this scientific law that the main premise of naturalism has been disproven—nature is not self-explanatory. We must proceed beyond nature for the explanation of its beginning. The universe can no longer be considered eternal, for the Second Law of Thermodynamics dictates that it requires an external source of energy and, further, that this source also maintains the universe.[30]

Scientist Robert E. D. Clark agrees in this assessment

---

[29]For some interesting observations on this subject from a scientific viewpoint, especially concerning the beginning of the universe, see Otto Blüh and Joseph D. Elder, *Principles and Applications of Physics* (New York: Interscience Publishers, Inc., 1955), pp. 474-475, 786-788, 808.
[30]Trueblood, *Philosophy of Religion*, pp. 102-105.

based on the Second Law of Thermodynamics. Since this law applies to the universe as a whole, it indicates that the universe is running down. If it is running down it cannot be eternal and must have been created. Such an act involves a creator, which is the mind behind the order and plan of the universe. Further, the evidence from the creation indicates that the creator is intelligent, has limitless power, and is interested in morality. Additionally, this creator is not a part of the creation but is beyond nature, sustaining it. As such, this scientific data defeats naturalism because a supernatural source for the universe is needed.[31]

These conclusions therefore point out that the universe was created at a point in time and, hence, a creator is necessitated. This creator is the cause of the universe. The intelligence, morality, and aesthetical nature of the creator are all revealed by the creation.

The philosophical argument from existential causality and the scientific argument from the Second Law of Thermodynamics are not presented here as rival theories. It is this author's belief that these theistic theories are compatible and can be utilized apologetically in complementary roles, although details cannot be enumerated at present.

The three theistic arguments presented in this chapter formulate a very strong case for theism. The other theistic arguments (teleological, moral, and ontological) thereby assume a new importance, especially in revealing even more about the nature of God. Further, in a theistic universe it is quite probable that God raised Jesus from the dead, since such an event would be in accordance with His attributes, as we will now perceive.

---

[31]For a defense of this position, including refutations of objections, see Robert E. D. Clark, *The Universe: Plan or Accident?* (London: The Paternoster Press, 1961; reprinted by Zondervan Publishing House, 1972), especially pp. 15–42, 192–236.

## Two Contrasting Paradigms

We may assert that, based on the evidence presented in Chapter I, the resurrection of Jesus is a verified historical event. Accordingly, it may be further stated that this event either occurred in a naturalistic universe or it occurred in a theistic universe.

The first paradigm option is that this event occurred in a naturalistic universe.[32] As such, God would not exist and the resurrection would have no known natural explanation and would thereby constitute a "freak event." Characteristically, such an oddity would simply be a random happening.

On the other hand, a second paradigm option dictates that the resurrection of Jesus occurred in a theistic universe. Here this event would be seen as an orderly act of God, performed in order to bring about a specific goal. As such, it would not be a random happening but would also be characterized by order, design, and purpose.

At this point it might be mentioned that both of these paradigm options often *assume* that their world view is correct. In other words, instead of having evidence which indicates which position is correct, a decision is too often based on assumptions.

For instance, the naturalistic paradigm often argues from the threefold position which assumes that God does not exist, that miracles do not occur, and that, therefore, Jesus' resurrection can have no actual interpretive significance in terms of theology. The problem here is that this position is often assumed to be true in spite of, and even contrary to, the facts. Thus, an investigation of the facts is

---

[32]A naturalist might, of course, hold that the resurrection of Jesus did not occur literally at all. However, this option is confronted with the various critiques and the corresponding evidences provided in Chapter I.

ruled out *a priori,* which, as pointed out earlier, is neither scientific nor historical.

Likewise, the theistic paradigm is also assumed many times, such as by the argument that the resurrection, as a "brute fact," carries with it certain theological interpretations. Some are too quick to proclaim the event a miracle, which, by definition, involves supernatural activity, just because it is an unexplainable event. Such a position assumes that God performed the event, based on its oddity. Stated briefly, the brute fact of a resurrection is taken to be an indication that God must have performed it, since no man could have done so.[33]

The problem with such views on the part of both parties is that their position is often assumed to be true. The odd event of the resurrection is judged by naturalists simply to be a "freak," while theists declare that the same event is so odd as to demand God's intervention.

The major question in this dilemma concerns which position best corresponds to the available factual data. It will be proposed here that the theistic paradigm is much superior to the naturalistic paradigm, not because it is an assumed position, but because an investigation reveals that it best fits the known data. Two major and independent reasons will be presented to back up this claim.

First, the theistic arguments such as those presented earlier show that this is indeed a theistic universe. Far from being assumed, these arguments provide an especially strong foundation to back this theistic claim, as they reveal that God really does exist. Then it is rational to conclude that in this orderly universe, the resurrection of Jesus was a purposeful event, performed by God in keeping with His known attributes. This occurrence can then provide an

---

[33]For a critique of such theistic assumptions, see Geisler, *Christian Apologetics,* pp. 95-97, 138-139.

answer to the question of which theism is correct. Therefore, the validity of theistic argumentation, the orderliness of the universe, and the literal resurrection are more in accordance with our second paradigm option above. Thus, arguing prospectively from theistic evidences to God's performing the resurrection of Jesus yields the most complete results on this question.

Second, although the brute fact of the resurrection cannot establish a world view by any inherent meaning, as we saw above, this event coupled with the claims of the person who was raised does provide other compelling reasons to accept a theistic universe as providing a better and more factual world view. Thus, the historical event plus the facts surrounding the Person and message of Jesus combine to show, once again, that the second paradigm option provides the most probable answer concerning the cause of this event.

As verified in the last section of this chapter, combining the historical event of the resurrection with the message of Jesus does make Jesus' theistic world view probable. Jesus claimed to be Deity and He also claimed to be fulfilling His Father's will in a very special sense by proclaiming a unique message. Are these claims valid? To verify them, Jesus performed miracles as a sign of His credibility. His resurrection from the dead, in particular, was singled out and predicted in advance to be the sign to vindicate His message and His own claim to Deity. These teachings constituted Jesus' belief in a theistic universe and He claimed that this view was verified by God's action in His resurrection. As an orderly event Jesus would best be able to interpret it. We therefore conclude that, according to probability, this unique historical event combined with Jesus' unique claims indicate that His theistic world view was validated.

The *converging nature* of this data presents a formidable

case in favor of the claimed theistic world view of Jesus. For instance, the chance or "freak event" claim of the naturalist is disposed of by Jesus' prior conviction of His mission, by the importance of His miracles, by His predictions of His resurrection, and by Jesus' theistic world view. As such, this event becomes a *planned occurrence* of which Jesus had foreknowledge, as was shown in Chapter 1. Additionally, it will be asserted below that what is known concerning Jesus' resurrection is at such odds with the laws of nature that such naturalistic chance hypotheses are dispelled.

It cannot be stressed enough that God is not being assumed by this second point, but, rather, that the literal resurrection plus the Person and message of Jesus reveal that God's action in this event is the most likely explanation. In short, this is a retrospective conclusion which reasons that, of the two possible choices, the proposed theistic paradigm best fits what is known of reality.

Thus, if some unknown "John Doe" had been raised from the dead, it might be called a freak event. But since such an occurrence happened *only* to the very Person who made the unique claims stated above, the probability is quite strongly in favor of this event providing *retrospective* corroboration of the theistic universe claimed by Jesus to be true.

Therefore, there is a difference between asserting that theism must be true as a prior condition and that we therefore assume theism. It is concluded that theism is valid not because of such an assumption, but because the facts back up this claim. In other words, given the two paradigms, the theistic universe is most consistent with the data. One may opt for other possibilities, but such are distinct improbabilities.

Therefore, having already provided a first argument for a theistic universe by proceeding *prospectively* from God's existence to the resurrection, we now turn to the details of our second argument, which proceeds *retrospectively* from the coupling of Jesus' resurrection with His Person and message to a theistic universe.

## Jesus' Unique Message

Arguing retrospectively from a combination of Jesus' resurrection, His Person, and His message to a theistic universe, several of Jesus' unique claims already mentioned must be investigated. It will be our endeavor to show that there is a high probability in favor of the conclusion that God did raise Jesus from the dead, thereby demanding a theistic universe.

### Jesus' Claim to Deity

It is only possible to outline this first argument, since it is more properly the subject of Chapter 3 and is substantiated there.[34] However, it does play a part in our discussion here, as well.

Jesus thought of Himself as Deity and referred to Himself that way many times. For instance, His *self-designations* (especially "Son of man" and "Son of God") reveal this conclusion quite strongly. They give us insight into Jesus' concept of Himself and His own nature. Another indication concerns Jesus' *claims to authority,* such as His being the only way to salvation and His assertions that His authority was greater than that of Jewish tradition and teaching.

Jesus' *actions* also convey this conclusion, especially in His exercising the power to forgive sin and His fulfillment of messianic prophecy, especially in cases where this could

---

[34]Along with our explication of these points, New Testament references will also be provided in Chapter 3.

not have been performed intentionally. Lastly, the *reactions* of others to the person of Jesus point to His Deity, such as His death, which was at least partially (if not primarily) due to His claims about Himself. Another response on the part of others was the apostolic testimony that Jesus was Deity. He is repeatedly called Lord, Christ, the Son of God, and even God.

Even this brief survey reveals that Jesus claimed to be Deity and that this designation was also applied to Him by others who were close to Him. In terms of our study, this is important since verification of Christ's claims would then verify a theistic universe, since Jesus Christ would be Deity Himself.

### Jesus' Mission

Second, Jesus claimed to be carrying out a mission on behalf of His Father, God. This is revealed in His personal conviction that He was speaking the words which God had delivered to Him.[35] As with His other claims, we will attempt to ascertain if this one is warranted by the facts.

Even critical theologians agree that Jesus was convinced that He was presenting God's unique message, especially concerning the kingdom of God, which was the center of His teaching.[36] For example, Fuller notes that in Jesus' preaching, men were confronted with God's message. In fact, Jesus believed that in His work, God was directly represented in His call for obedience, salvation and judgment.[37] Bultmann likewise notes that Jesus believed that in His own Person and message were brought the tidings of

---

[35] Jesus spoke of His mission often (cf. Mark 2:17; 10:45; 14:22–25; Luke 19:10; 22:29, for instance), being convicted that He spoke God's words (see Matt. 11:27; Luke 10:22; John 8:26, 42; 12:49–50; 13:3).
[36] We will return to this latter point in Chapter 3.
[37] See Reginald H. Fuller, *The Foundations of New Testament Christology* (New York: Charles Scribner's Sons, 1965), especially pp. 105–106.

God's kingdom.[38] Pannenberg concurs that Jesus revealed God like no other man had and that in His Person and message God was revealing Himself to men in a unique way.[39]

Not only did Jesus preach God's message of the kingdom in a unique way, He also believed that His miracles were a sign that God approved of His teachings.[40] Critical theologians likewise recognize and accept the fact that Jesus believed and taught that His miracles were an evidence of God's working in Him and through His teachings.[41]

It is most significant that Jesus claimed that He was God's chief revelation to men, also believing that in His message God was confronting mankind with His kingdom.[42] It is equally important that Jesus believed that His miracles were evidence of God's power in Him and that these occurrences were also divine indications of God's approval. In light of the reality of the resurrection, which was already shown to be a historical event, could it only have been an accident that Jesus was raised from the dead?

Either Jesus spoke the truth about His Person and message and God did vindicate Him by the grand miracle of raising Him from the dead, or Jesus' resurrection involved at least three "coincidences" which combine to produce a high degree of improbability. First, Jesus proclaimed a unique message, especially concerning His relationship to

---

[38]See Bultmann, *Theology of the New Testament,* volume I, pp. 4-11.

[39]See Pannenberg's essay "Dogmatic Theses on the Doctrine of Revelation" in *Revelation As History,* edited by Pannenberg, translated by David Granskou (New York: The Macmillan Company, 1968), pp. 139-145 for instance.

[40]See, for instance, Mark 2:1-12; Matt. 11:1-6; 12:22-28; John 5:36-37; 10:36-38; cf. Acts 2:22-24; Heb. 2:3-4.

[41]For examples, see Bultmann, *Theology of the New Testament,* volume I, p. 7; Fuller, *The Foundations of New Testament Christology,* p. 107; Pannenberg, *Jesus—God and Man,* p. 64.

[42]For a noteworthy evangelical discussion of these teachings, see George E. Ladd, *The Pattern of New Testament Truth* (Grand Rapids: William B. Eerdman's Publishing Company, 1968), pp. 41-63.

God.[43] Second, Jesus claimed that His miracles were a sign of God's approval, later being literally raised from the dead. Third, His resurrection has never since been duplicated.

That Jesus' resurrection has never been repeated gives us an important pointer to the existence and work of God. This is because the only time that such an event was ever known to have occurred, it "happened" to be the one who most uniquely believed that He Himself was Deity, that He was God's chosen messenger, and that God was verifying His message by miracles.

Here we have a second retrospective reason for believing both that God exists and that He acted in raising Jesus from the dead. The most unique messenger in history personally experienced the most unique event in history. Such a combination, especially in light of Jesus' view of miracles being done by God and the fact that the resurrection has never been duplicated since leads us to conclude that it was God who raised Jesus from the dead. It is thus probable that, just as Jesus claimed, God vindicated His teachings by raising Him from the dead.

## Jesus' Predictions of His Resurrection

The third indication that God was the one who intervened in history to raise Jesus from the dead is that Jesus specifically predicted His coming resurrection.[44] Critical theology recognizes that Jesus knew that He was going to die,[45] but it generally denies that Jesus predicted His resurrection.

---

[43]See J. N. D. Anderson, *Christianity and Comparative Religion* (Downer's Grove: Inter Varsity Press, 1970) for the uniqueness of Christ and His message among the world's religions, especially regarding His death and resurrection.

[44]See Mark 8:31; 9:31; 10:33, 34; 14:27, 28; Matt. 12:38-40; John 2:18-22.

[45]For instance, see Fuller, *The Foundations of New Testament Christology*, pp. 107-108; Bornkamm, *Jesus of Nazareth*, pp. 154-155; Millar Burrows, *An Outline of Biblical Theology* (Philadelphia: The Westminster Press, 1946), pp. 222-223.

We would assert that there are at least three reasons to accept Jesus' predictions as historical. First, these predictions are usually denied not only because of their prophetic nature, but also because the resurrection is likewise denied. Thus, the predictions are often rejected because the literal event is rejected.

But since the resurrection has already been shown to be a literal historical event, it is plainly illogical to reject the predictions of this event. For instance, one should no longer object to the prophetic and supernatural nature of the predictions since the resurrection itself, surely a greater event, is already shown to be historical. If the greater be historical, why not the lesser?

Second, there is a good textual consideration which points to the historicity of these predictions. Usually when Jesus spoke of His coming death and being raised afterwards, the disciples misunderstood. Jesus' announcement in Mark 8:31 predicates Peter's objection to this fate, bringing Jesus' rebuke of Peter. In Mark 9:31 Jesus issues a similar announcement, and we are then informed that the disciples did not understand. In Mark 14:27-28 Jesus predicts His future and Peter again objects, followed by Jesus' statement that Peter would deny Him three times.

After Jesus rose from the dead, the gospels once again agree that the disciples did not understand. We are told that, in spite of Jesus' specific command to meet Him in Galilee after His resurrection (Mark 14:27-28), the disciples still had to be reminded of this later (Mark 16:7,8; Matt. 28:7). We are further told in Luke 24:21 and John 20:9 that the disciples did not know that Jesus was to rise from the dead.

In all of these instances we perceive that the disciples were plainly placed in a negative light. They did not understand Jesus' predictions and even reacted against them.

If these predictions were not factual, why would they be recorded under these disfavorable conditons? Would not the early church want the disciples to appear in a positive light? An interesting factor here is that Peter, the traditional source behind the Gospel of Mark and the leader of the disciples, appears in an especially negative way in this gospel.

Since the resurrection predictions of Jesus serve no real apologetic value in the gospels or in the early church and since they were not conditioned by the Jewish milieu, we thereby have a good indication that these proclamations are historical, even by critical methodology.[46] At any rate, the disciples' ignorance and lack of understanding is another indicator that Jesus' predictions are genuine.

The third argument in favor of the authenticity of Jesus' predictions of His coming resurrection is utilized by such scholars as Oscar Cullmann and George E. Ladd. The argument concerns Jesus' use of the term "Son of man" in Mark 8:31; 9:31; 10:33-34.[47]

Most scholars agree that the gospel concept of "Son of man" is set against a background of pre-Christian Jewish apocalypticism. Here the Son of man was believed to be a heavenly being, both preexistent and divine, who would come from heaven in the last days to deliver the elect, judge the wicked and set up and rule the kingdom of God for eternity.[48]

As we saw, Jesus connected the ideas of suffering, dying,

---

[46]See James M. Robinson, *A New Quest of the Historical Jesus* (London: SCM Press, Ltd., 1959), p. 99.

[47]The contemporary theological literature on the "Son of man sayings" is voluminous. For a reputable treatment, see Oscar Cullmann, *The Christology of the New Testament*, translated by Shirley C. Guthrie and Charles A. M. Hall (Philadelphia: The Westminster Press, 1963), pp. 137-192.

[48]See Cullmann, Ibid., pp. 137-152; Fuller, *The Foundations of New Testament Christology*, pp. 34-43; George E. Ladd, *I Believe in the Resurrection of Jesus* (Grand Rapids: William B. Eerdman's Publishing Company, 1975), pp. 64-66.

and rising again with the Son of man figure. But this was a new concept. The Jews believed that the Son of man was to conquer God's enemies and rule His kingdom, not die and be raised again. Thus we find that this was offensive to the disciples (Mark 8:32) and they failed to understand (Mark 9:33). It is little wonder that Jesus' predictions did not prepare them for His death and resurrection.

Further, the early church never used "Son of man" to describe the earthly ministry of Jesus, as far as we know. It is not used in Paul's writings or in the other New Testament epistles. Rather, in the gospels, the Son of man is always a designate of Jesus when referring to Himself.

Therefore, this concept of the suffering Son of man is so unique that it must have originated with Jesus, especially when we find that the church does not use it of Him. To say that the church invented these sayings is very odd, both because they do not do it elsewhere and because the very idea was offensive and foreign to them. The conclusion here is that these predictions of Jesus' death and subsequent resurrection are original sayings of Jesus.[49]

For these three reasons, then, it is probable that Jesus actually did predict His own resurrection. The historical reality of the resurrection itself, the improbability that the church used defamatory data concerning the disciples without any clear apologetic for doing so, and Jesus' use of "Son of man" concepts pertaining to Himself all point to the validity of these predictions.

That Jesus predicted His own resurrection clearly shows that this event was not simply a coincidence or a chance occurrence. Rather, Jesus' pre-knowledge of this event and His ability to speak of it ahead of time as an act of God shows that the resurrection was, according to probability, a

---

[49]See Ladd, Ibid., pp. 35-36, 70-72; Cullman, Ibid., p. 63.

planned event performed by God. Jesus also claimed that this occurrence was the chief verification of His message (see Matt. 12:38–40, John 2:18–22). So, once again, we perceive that Jesus' resurrection involves the existence of God and His action in history.

## Jesus' Theistic World View

Before turning to our last point concerning the relationship between Jesus' resurrection and the laws of nature, a word should be said about Jesus' theistic world view. Such is an obvious point especially in light of the foregoing discussion here.

Jesus claimed to be Deity, which, if vindicated, would mean that the universe is theistic, since He Himself was Divine. In addition, it was pointed out how Jesus was convinced that He was fulfilling His Father's will by bringing a unique message to mankind, verified by miracles and by His resurrection in particular. In both instances, whether Jesus was speaking of Himself or His Father, a theistic universe was being taught.

Thus, especially in light of Jesus' conviction that He was presenting a unique message and in view of His predictions that He would rise again, we find that the resurrection was an orderly and planned occurrence. As such, it is reasonable that Jesus would best be able to explain the purpose behind the event itself. His testimony is that, as the chief miracle, this event was the sign that His world view was verified by an act of God. As already mentioned, the only known time that a resurrection has ever taken place it occurred to the only Person who made these unique claims about His own Deity, His special message and who taught that God verified these claims by his miracles. In short, His unique message as a whole combined with the unique resurrection event make it probable that His claims concerning His theistic world view were validated.[50]

Therefore, Jesus' mission and His claims are especially valuable in that He was literally raised from the dead. We judge that, according to probability, His theistic world view was thereby shown to be correct.

## The Resurrection and the Laws of Nature

A miracle is, by definition, a violation or interference with the laws of nature, brought about by the action of God.[51] But how do we ascertain when such an occurrence does interfere with these laws?

Probably the clearest example of a violation of the laws of nature would be the occurrence of a nonrepeatable phenomenon or event which runs counter to an established law.[52] This is not to say that such instances could never occur more than once, if caused by the action of God. However, the nonrepeatable phenomenon is easier to evaluate, as we will perceive.

In contrast to a nonrepeatable occurrence, those which appear to violate a law but happen regularly under certain circumstances would indicate that a supposed law was not really a law of nature. Thus, if a phenomenon could regularly be induced it would mean that the law would need to be adjusted or changed in order to account for its occurrence under those conditions.

Having said this, how do we know when (or if) miracles

---

[50]See Matt. 12:38–40; John 2:18–22 and Sections D-1 through D-3 above.
[51]This definition is a well-accepted one. See Hume, "Of Miracles," Section X of *An Enquiry Concerning Human Understanding;* Lewis, *Miracles,* p. 10; cf. Habermas, *The Resurrection of Jesus: A Rational Inquiry,* pp. 26–29.
[52]See Swinburne, *The Concept of Miracle,* p. 26, who additionally notes that this is the concept held by Hume and others dealing with this subject.

have occurred? We would suggest the use of a few criteria which have already been suggested above.

It should be determined whether an event runs counter to a law(s) of nature or not. Next, does the event continue to occur under certain circumstances? If so, it should be ascertained if the law either needs adjusting or if another law needs to be formulated to take its place.

However, there can also be indications that the original law is the correct expression of this rule. For example, that the law works in all situations except in this one instance is an important pointer to its validity. Or the new law might be too unworkable due to adjustments and qualifications. Lastly, a new law covering the event in question may be virtually impossible to formulate, since the occurrence so strongly contradicts what is known about reality.[53]

Therefore, it is increasingly possible that an event would be a miracle, and hence a violation of (or interference with) the laws of nature, if it fulfilled these criteria. The best case could be made for an occurrence which was nonrepeatable and which ran counter to a law of nature concerning which this was the only exception to that law. The case for this violation would be made even stronger if no known law could be made to allow for this deviation.

Some might respond that some day the law might change and then the exception to it would also change. At least two responses to this are possible. First, this could be said about virtually all our knowledge concerning the physical world. But it is plain that we cannot suspend knowledge because of such future considerations. We must decide and act on our present knowledge. Second, it is probable that most of our better established laws will never change. For instance, there never was any hope of restoring people to life who were actually dead, once the

---

[53]Cf. Ibid., pp. 26-27, 31.

irreversible process began. This is not likely to change in the future.[54]

After a similar investigation of the laws of nature, Swinburne concludes that certain occurrences can be given as examples of events which, if they happened, could be said to violate the laws of nature. Such instances would include a resurrection of a dead man who had been dead for at least one day, water changing to wine without the use of chemicals or catalysts, or a man recovering from polio in one minute. We know enough about such events to be fairly certain in our judgment that these are physically impossible happenings.[55]

We conclude here that the resurrection of Jesus is not only an example of such an interference with nature's laws, but that it is the best example of such an occurrence. It fulfills the criteria set forth above. It was a nonrepeatable event and did indeed violate the law which dictates that an irreversible process like death cannot be changed so that a fully dead person can be returned to life by natural means. As far as we know, Jesus' resurrection is the only exception to a law which has otherwise claimed a countless number of lives.

Neither is there any way to modify or expand this law of life and death or to substitute a new law for it. As was mentioned above, some events cannot be allowed for by any law. Jesus' resurrection is such an event. Fully dead men simply do not rise by any natural process. This is one of our most universal laws.

That no law can be made to account for this event is further demonstrated by the manner in which Jesus rose from the dead. He returned in a supernatural, spiritual body with powers which also transcended natural laws, as

---

[54]Ibid., p. 31.
[55]Ibid., p. 32. For similar points, see R. F. Holland's essay "The Miraculous" in Donnelly, *Logical Analysis and Contemporary Theism*, pp. 218-235.

indicated by the same eyewitness testimony which we investigated in Chapter 1. This separates His resurrection from resuscitations.[56]

We saw above that miracles are defined as occurrences which run counter to the laws of nature and which are brought about by God. In asserting that Jesus' resurrection is a miracle and ·thus an interference with the laws of nature, we thereby conclude our fifth argument that God was the one who performed this event. Several reasons indicated that this conclusion was correct.

We found, to summarize briefly, not only that the resurrection was contrary to these laws, but that it was a nonrepeatable event. It is also the only exception to these laws in history. Additionally, adjusting the laws or formulating new ones still would not allow for this event.

But not only did Jesus rise from the dead, He also returned in a new body with new powers, as indicated by the eyewitnesses. Since nature cannot account for such a transformation, we have an especially strong indication that such was not a freak occurrence, but an event performed by God. It is noteworthy here that even David Hume admitted that the resurrection of a dead man would be a miracle, involving supernatural intervention.[57]

A further indication that it was only by the existence and power of God that Jesus was raised was already given in our first four arguments concerning Christ's Deity, mission, prophecy of His being raised from the dead, and overall theistic world view. When combined, these five present a formidable basis for our conclusion that God

---

[56]As will be even more apparent below, we are differentiating between Jesus' resurrection and those who have returned to their former earthly life after death. The difference is that, according to eyewitness testimony, Jesus rose in a new spiritual body characterized by new powers (see especially Appendix 3, Section A-4).

[57]Hume, "Of Miracles," Section X of *An Enquiry Concerning Human Understanding*.

acted in the resurrection as a purposeful, planned and unprecedented event. He performed this act on behalf of Jesus by working in man's history.

## Conclusion

In this chapter we began with an investigation of the tenets of logical positivism and linguistic analysis. Because of several critiques we found that these philosophies were unable to rule out "God-talk," miracles such as the resurrection or the meaningfulness of Christian theology. In fact, we even buttressed our apologetic for Jesus' resurrection by showing that this event could be demonstrated to be a time-space, empirical event.

Next we briefly viewed the question of theistic argumentation, looking specifically at three arguments. C. S. Lewis concluded that if rational thinking is valid, a rational mind must exist to account for it since an irrational beginning cannot allow us to *know* anything for sure. Norman Geisler provided a very strong cosmological argument from existential causality, which argued that if any finite beings exist, an infinite being must exist in order to account for finite life. We also viewed the Second Law of Thermodynamics, which teaches that the universe is running down towards greater entropy. Since the universe is therefore not eternal, this provides a strong reason for concluding that it must have been "wound up" at some time in the past by a source outside of itself.

After viewing the naturalistic and supernatural paradigms as possible options for the world in which Jesus' resurrection occurred, it was concluded that the supernatural paradigm was superior. Two main arguments were given to show God's existence and involvement in raising Jesus.

First, theistic arguments show that a theistic paradigm is

the most probable option. As such, we may argue *prospectively* from God's existence to Jesus' resurrection, since in a theistic universe it is very probable that God raised Jesus in an orderly, purposeful manner, in accordance with His attributes.

Second, we argued *retrospectively* by combining Jesus' resurrection with several of His claims. For instance, Jesus claimed to be Deity by His self-designations, by His claims to authority, by His actions, and by other's reactions to Him. Such indicates His belief in a theistic universe.

We also saw that Jesus claimed to be the special messenger of God sent to present a chosen message and believing that His miracles were a sign of God's corroboration of His ministry. That such a unique messenger was also uniquely raised from the dead, especially in view of Jesus' understanding of the miraculous, is a very probable indicator that it was God who raised Him from the dead.

Additionally, Jesus prophesied His own resurrection ahead of time as the major verification of His message. That He was able to do so convincingly shows that God performed this event in an orderly fashion and that Jesus had foreknowledge of it.

Yet another extremely important point concerns Jesus' personal theistic world view. His unique message, His view concerning His corroborating miracles and His predicted resurrection point to this event as an orderly and planned occurrence. Therefore, Jesus would have the best perspective concerning the resurrection and would best be able to interpret it. He taught that it vindicated His message and His personal claims. His theistic world view was further judged to be valid especially since the only time that a resurrection is known to have occurred, it happened to the only Person who made these most unique claims concerning both Himself and God. We thus found that, according to probability, the resurrection vindicated Jesus' theistic world view.

Lastly, we saw that Jesus' resurrection was a miracle, meaning that it was an event which God accomplished by suspending the laws of nature. This is indicated in that the resurrection occurred contrary to these laws of life and death, was nonrepeatable, and was the only such violation of these laws in history. Also, the laws cannot be modified or changed in order to account for this event. Coupled with Jesus' new spiritual body having special powers not accounted for by nature and the noncoincidental characteristics of this event, we thereby affirm God's existence and performance of the resurrection.

It should be mentioned here that of our two paradigms in which the resurrection could have occurred, the *converging data* of our retrospective argument is strictly in keeping with the occurrence of this event in a theistic universe. Jesus preached a unique message, especially concerning His Deity and His relationship to God. He claimed that miracles were the sign of God's approval and that His resurrection was the chief sign vindicating His theistic world view and corresponding message. In light of these facts, it is very significant that Jesus was the *only* Person ever known who made such claims *and* rose from the dead.

Thus, when the literal resurrection is combined with Jesus' unique Person and message, we find a vindication of His theistic world view, according to probability. As such, this event was orderly and performed by God in a theistic universe for a certain purpose—to corroborate the Person and teachings of His Son. This latter point (concerning God's vindication of Jesus' Person and teachings as a *whole*) will be the main subject of our next chapter.[58]

---

[58]One of our main theses in this book is that God, through the resurrection, verified Jesus' message, both concerning His own Person and other areas of His teaching. In the second major argument in this chapter we stressed how this thereby vindicated Jesus' theistic world view. In Chapter 3 we turn to the truthfulness of Jesus' *entire* message based on His resurrection.

Our two major arguments presented in this chapter are capable, both individually and independently, of ascertaining both the probability of God's existence and His action in Jesus' resurrection. But together they present a much stronger converging demonstration of God and His activity in this event.

We therefore conclude not only that the resurrection occurred in literal history (Chapter 1), but also that God performed this event, thus demanding His existence and action in a theistic universe. We may thus affirm, in light of our study, that God did temporarily set aside the laws of nature in order to bring about this miracle.

We will illustrate the first two steps of our apologetic as follows:

## STEP 2

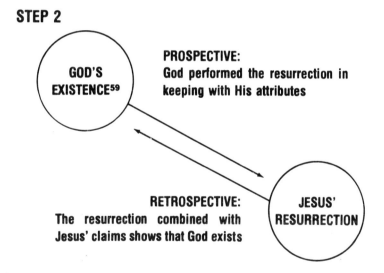

**PROSPECTIVE:**
**God performed the resurrection in keeping with His attributes**

**GOD'S EXISTENCE**[59]

**JESUS' RESURRECTION**

**RETROSPECTIVE:**
**The resurrection combined with Jesus' claims shows that God exists**

---

[59]The second step in the illustration of our apologetic is *not* to subordinate God to the resurrection in any way. This would most assuredly be incorrect. God's existence was obviously prior to this event, as indicated both by the downward arrow and by the elevated position of the second step. Rather, our diagram indicates that we are beginning with Jesus' resurrection.

# CHAPTER THREE

# The Person and Teachings
# of Christ

We established in our first two chapters both that Jesus literally rose from the dead in history and that God exists and performed this act. Now we must ascertain more fully what these facts indicate with regards to the Person and teachings of Jesus Christ.

## A Key Principle

We saw above that Jesus was convinced that He was Deity, that He was God's chosen messenger and that in Him, God was confronting mankind with the teachings of the kingdom. Not only did Jesus believe that He was presenting the specific message which God had delivered to Him, but He also taught that His miracles were a sign of God's approval of His message. Even critical theology accepts these facts.[1]

---

[1] Willi Marxsen, in his work *The Resurrection of Jesus of Nazareth*, translated by Margaret Kohl (Philadelphia: Fortress Press, 1970), pp. 125, 169, speaks for

We also saw that Jesus predicted His resurrection as the chief evidence for His words and that this event, as the greatest miracle, was the supreme vindication of Jesus' message by God. By raising Jesus from the dead, God was placing final approval on that message and thereby validated Jesus' view of the theistic universe.

Other alternative options with regard to God's action in Jesus' resurrection are all quite improbable. If Christ's teachings were not correct or if another religion presented the proper way to God, why was Christ raised, especially in light of His exclusive message that He was the only way to God? As shown in the last chapter, the resurrection confirms Christ's message, thus eliminating these two options. Or if all religions are valid ways to God, why were not the other great religious founders also raised from the dead so that we might know that their messages were similarly true? Again, Christ's exclusivistic proclamations likewise disprove this position.

Could God simply have been acting illogically or even purposely in order to confuse man? Such views must be rejected for several different reasons. These alternatives would not be in keeping with the character of God. Also, we saw that His attributes gained from the theistic arguments militate very strongly against any deception. For instance, the moral character of God contradicts such action. Additionally, there is a real logical consistency in

---

many critical theologians by looking for significance in the resurrection and finding that God acknowledged Jesus and his teachings through it. Marxsen rejects the literal teachings of Jesus in many areas, but this is because he also rejects the literal resurrection. But here critical theology has a dilemma. One might reject the literal Deity of Christ and other teachings of Jesus, wrongly believing that Jesus did not literally rise from the dead. But when the resurrection is shown to be a real historical event, are we not then on firm grounds to accept these other doctrines literally, as well? If the doctrine relies on the event which is widely recognized by critical theologians, then should we not accept the literal doctrine if the event is literal? In this chapter we will examine this relationship between Jesus' resurrection and His teachings.

Christian theism, such as in God's actions in Jesus which confirmed Jesus' theistic world view, which oppose such illogical motives. We also find that those who have responded to Jesus' promises, based on the above objective data, indicate that God keeps His promises. Lastly, such illogical views are only idle ventures in that no evidence supports such claims.

As in other matters, we have to decide questions based on the available evidence; converging evidence indicates that these options are therefore inadequate to account for the facts. The character of God such as that which is gained from theistic arguments and from our other studies, combined with the logical character of Jesus' conviction concerning His message and God's subsequent validating actions in raising Him from the dead, plus the continuing testimony of believers who have acted upon the reality of these objective events and who have found God faithful, all demonstrate the futility of such alternative explanations. Such alternate hypotheses concerning God's actions are devoid of evidence anyway.

Therefore, we can ascertain that God had a specific purpose in raising Jesus. Such is consistent with His nature. Since this event was not a coincidence or a freak occurrence of nature and since God performed it, both of which were shown above, we know that God thereby was in agreement with Jesus' teaching.

This brings us to a key principle in this work. *By raising Jesus from the dead, God placed His stamp of approval on Jesus' entire message, both concerning His Person and including His other teachings, because God would not have raised a heretic from the dead.* Such a principle is based on the facts we have discussed above.

There is actually a two-fold reason for the acceptance of this principle. Positively, God acted consistently with His nature by raising Jesus from the dead. Both the prospective and retrospective arguments presented in Chapter 2 verify this conclusion. God's act signified an approval of Jesus' total message, which we separated into Jesus' teachings concerning His Person and His teaching in other areas.

Negatively, raising a heretic would be contrary to God's nature for the same reasons we gave above. If Jesus was a false teacher, God would not have placed His stamp of approval on the whole message, as he did by raising Jesus.

One reason that this principle is so important is that it opens us up to a study of Jesus' Person and His other teachings. In determining Jesus' message on these issues, we can additionally know that we have the truth, based on God's approval of them. We will turn to such a study now.

## God's Approval of Jesus' Person

We just concluded that God approved of both Jesus' teachings concerning His own Person and His teaching in other areas. Thus we will turn now to Jesus' words concerning His own Person. Even though Jesus never specifically called Himself God in the New Testament,[2] there are at least eight other very strong indications that He thought of Himself as Deity.

First, Jesus' favorite designation for Himself was "Son of man" (Mark 2:10-11; 10:45). As we noted in Chapter 2, this concept is rooted in the Jewish apocalyptic ideas of pre-Christian times (cf. Dan. 7:13-14, for instance). The Son of man was believed to be a pre-existent divine personage who would be hidden until the time of the end. At such time he would deliver God's elect, judge the wicked

---

[2]Even in statements like John 10:30, "I and the Father are One", Jesus is not specifically designating Himself as "God" (cf. John 1:1; 20:28, etc.).

and set up the rule of God's kingdom. The person of the Son of man was linked with messiahship.

The majority of critical scholars hold that Jesus used this title personally in order to substantiate His messianic claims. Some critics, however, do hold that this designation was given to Him by the early church, thus reflecting a later theology.[3]

In answer to this second opinion, Cullmann gives a strong refutation. Holding that such a view is too simplistic, Cullmann asks how the early church could have given this title to the earthly Jesus when they never call Him this at all. For example, "Son of man" does not appear in Paul's writings or in any other New Testament epistle. Outside of the gospels, only Acts 7:56 and Rev. 1:13 use this title and even in both of these instances it is applied to the heavenly, glorified Christ. Furthermore, Jesus is never called this by anyone else in the gospels. It is strictly a self-designation. It would be good to remember our earlier conclusion as well, which dictates that the idea of a *suffering* Son of man was so novel that it had to have originated with Jesus because of its offence to Jews.

Such information reveals that the early church did not invent this title for Jesus, especially since Jesus is never referred to in this way pertaining to His earthly ministry by anyone except Himself. Rather, it is much more probable that Jesus originally applied this title to Himself, as recorded in the gospels.

In concluding that "Son of man" was indeed a self-designation of Jesus, we may assert that it gives us important insight into His teachings about His Person. Definite references are thus being made to such truths as His

---

[3]Both Bultmann (*Theology of the New Testament*, volume I, p. 26) and Bornkamm (*Jesus of Nazareth*, p. 230) admit that they are in the minority, yet they take the latter position.

former heavenly dwelling and pre-existence and even to His Deity.[4]

Second, Jesus also referred to Himself as the Son of God. There are both direct references which claim this title (see Mark 13:32; Matt. 11:27; etc.) and other indications that Jesus claimed a special relationship to God which no one else had.

For instance, Jesus referred to God as *Abba* (see Mark 14:36), the Aramaic word for "Daddy". No other Jewish teachers used this title to describe Jehovah. Other studies of Jesus' references to God also reveal His belief that He stood in a special relationship to Him.[5]

The title "Son of God" is even more obviously an indication of Jesus' Deity, as are the personal references to God as His Father. It is noteworthy here that in first century thought, the title "Son of God" was a statement of equality to God the Father (John 5:18).

In addition to Christological titles, there are other indications of Jesus' conviction of His Deity. Out third argument for believing that He made this claim was that the chief reason He was slandered and finally killed was that He was placing Himself in a position of Deity (Mark 14:61-63). Thus, His claims to being in a special relationship to God were taken to be blasphemy by some of His listeners. Once again, we are told that some of these people thought Jesus was claiming equality with God (John 5:18).[6]

A fourth indication that Jesus claimed the position of Deity was His conviction that salvation was found only in

---

[4]See Cullmann, *The Christology of the New Testament*, pp. 155, 162-164, 182, 302. Cf. Ladd, *I Believe in the Resurrection of Jesus*, pp. 35-36 for a similarly stated conclusion.

[5]See Cullmann, Ibid., pp. 270-290, especially pp. 281, 289, 290; Raymond E. Brown, *Jesus: God and Man* (Milwaukee: The Bruce Publishing Company, 1967), pp. 76, 86-93; cf. Fuller, *The Foundations of New Testament Christology*, pp. 114-115.

[6]See Fuller, Ibid., pp. 110, 135; Pannenberg, *Jesus—God and Man,* p. 67.

Himself. His central message proclaimed that He was God's instrument of salvation for mankind. How a man would fare at judgment and whether he would participate in everlasting life in the eternal kingdom of God rested on his personal relationship to Jesus (Mark 8:34-38; Matt. 19:28-29; John 6:46). In such a way Jesus believed that God was directly ·present in His preaching, confronting men with the need for a personal decision on their part. Salvation was offered to those who responded in accordance with Jesus' directives.[7]

Fifth, Jesus asserted His power to forgive sins (Mark 2:1-12). The Jewish scribes correctly perceived that in so doing, Jesus was acting in a way that was a prerogative of God alone. He was guilty of blasphemy unless He was, indeed, God. Jesus responded by claiming this authority to perform this act.[8]

During His entire earthly ministry we see a sixth indication of Jesus' Deity in His exercise of authority in other areas. He continually challenged Jewish tradition and interpretation, claiming to be a superior authority (Mark 3:1-6; Matt. 5:20-48 for examples). Once again, in these and other respects Jesus claimed the very authority of God.[9]

A seventh indication that Jesus conceived of Himself as the Messiah and chosen one of God was His fulfillment of Old Testament prophecy. This is seen on many occasions, such as His conviction that He was the suffering servant of

---

[7]Fuller, Ibid., pp. 105-106; Brown, *Jesus: God and Man*, pp. 99, 101; Pannenberg, Ibid., pp. 61, 64; cf. Bultmann, *Theology of the New Testament*, volume I, pp. 9-10.

[8]Cullman, *The Christology of the New Testament*, p. 154.

[9]See Pannenberg, *Jesus—God and Man*, p. 56, in regard to Ernst Kasemann's citing of Jesus' authority; cf. Bornkamm, *Jesus of Nazareth*, pp. 97, 99. For an excellent discussion of Jesus' authority as presented in Matt. 5, see R. Laird Harris, *Inspiration and Canonicity of the Bible* (Grand Rapids: Zondervan Publishing House, 1957), pp. 46-57.

Isaish 53.[10] Predicted events such as Jesus' birth in Bethlehem (Micah 5:2; cf. Luke 2:1-6, complete with historical data), the specific time of His death (Dan. 9:24-27), the events involved (Isa. 53) and His resurrection and exaltation (Ps. 16:10; Isa. 52: 13-15) are extremely important because these were occurrences which could not have been manipulated. We should also note that Isa. 9:6, 7 also predicted Deity of the coming Messiah. By the fulfillment of these prophecies, Jesus linked Himself with the Old Testament Messiah to be sent by God, and, especially in the case of Isa. 9:6, 7, thereby took the name of Deity.

The eighth indication that Jesus was Deity is the apostolic witness to Jesus' Person. Those who were repeatedly with Him and who passed His message on to others understood that Jesus was claiming Deity. That they were in the best position to understand Jesus' teaching in this area additionally makes the apostolic witness a very important one. For example, Jesus was referred to unequivocally as the Son of God in this early testimony (cf. John 20:31; Rom. 15:6; Heb. 1:5; I Peter 1:3; etc.), a title we have already investigated and one which is certainly connected with Deity.

The designation *Lord* was commonly given to Jesus in the early Christian community. Early creeds such as Rom. 1:3, 4 and Phil. 2:7-11 apply this title to Jesus, as do a variety of other New Testament verses. An important consequence of this title is that Jesus was more closely associated with God the Father. Old Testament passages referring specifically to God were applied directly to Jesus, referring to Him as Lord (cf. Isa. 45:23 with Phil. 2:10-11;

---

[10]See Cullman's treatment (*The Christology of the New Testament*, pp. 60-82), including the aspect of Jesus' fulfillment of prophecy (Ibid., pp. 317-318). Cf. Peter Stoner, *Science Speaks* (Revised edition; Chicago: Moody Press, 1968), pp. 99-112.

Ps. 102:25-27 with Heb. 1:10-12 for instances of this). Jesus was being identified with Deity.[11]

The title *Christ* (or Messiah) is also given to Jesus many times, such as in the early Christian creeds in I Cor. 15:3ff., Rom. 1:3, 4 and Phil. 2:7-11, for instance. This would also serve to relate Old Testament messianic prophecy to Him. We already saw how Isa. 9:6, 7 referred to the coming Messiah as Deity.

It was also in the epistles that Jesus was *specifically* referred to as God. Of the many passages which possibly make this equation, several are obscured both by variant readings and by the question of whether it is God the Father or Christ who is being referred to.

Nonetheless, theologians are agreed that there are several references in which Jesus is positively called God (such as John 1:1; 20:28; Heb. 1:8). Other passages can also be said, in all probability, to call Jesus God (such as John 1:18; Rom. 9:5; Titus 2:13; II Peter 1:1; I John 5:20).[12] At any rate, there are about eight passages in the New Testament which give Jesus the highest possible title, that of God.

It should be mentioned here that while Jesus therefore viewed Himself as Deity and as the early church also applied such titles to Him, it is also clear that Jesus is placed in a subordinate position to God the Father. Such instances occur both in Jesus' words (Mark 13:32; John 14:28; 20:17; etc.) and in the early church (I Cor. 11:3; 15:24-28; Eph. 1:17; I Peter 1:3; etc.).

At this point we must be very careful. From the third to the fifth centuries, in particular, "subordinationism" became a heresy in that it made Jesus a creature and less than

---

[11]Cullmann, Ibid., pp. 234-237.
[12]For key studies on such verses, see Cullmann, Ibid., pp. 306-314; Brown, *Jesus: God and Man*, pp. 10-28.

God in terms of Deity. This most notably appears in the writings of Arius.

Therefore, statements concerning the subordinacy of Christ must be balanced with those referring to Him as Deity. It is this author's view that Col. 2:9 forms a pivotal point here (cf. Col. 1:19). Paul claims that the fulness of Deity (πλήρωμα τῆς θεότητος) dwells in Christ.[13] Based on this, we might state that to subordinate Christ's Deity is incorrect, since the fulness of Deity resided in Him. Yet His position is subordinate to that of God.

In studying the gospels we find that this view is substantiated. John tells us that Jesus repeatedly acknowledged that He was subordinate in position. Jesus was sent by God (John 8:42). His words were His Father's, who also performed His works through Him (John 14:10). It is even related that Jesus could do nothing by Himself. Rather, He reproduced the works which He had seen God do (John 5:19), accomplishing those things which God had given Him to carry out (John 5:36; 10:18; cf. Luke 22:29).[14]

Note that these references have to do with Jesus' *obedience* to His Father and pertains to His *reliance* upon God for His words and works, thus showing a subordination of position. Such is also the best conclusion when we recall that Jesus was full Deity. Lest someone conclude that this subordination applies only to the earthly Jesus, we should note the New Testament statements to the contrary, especially in I Cor. 15:24–28, which deals with the eternal relationship between Jesus Christ and His Father (cf. I Cor. 11:3; II Cor. 1:3, etc.).

---

[13]See W. E. Vine, *An Expository Dictionary of New Testament Words* (Four volumes; Old Tappan: Fleming H. Revell Company, 1966), vol. I, pp. 328–329.
[14]See also John 6:29, 57; 8:26, 29, 40. It is interesting to note that the New Testament book which calls Jesus *God* most frequently also stresses this subordinacy most. For John, there was no contradiction, as these concepts were compatible.

We therefore conclude that Jesus taught that He was Deity. He did this by the titles He used of Himself, by His claims to authority, and by His actions. The reactions of others, such as the Jewish authorities and the early apostolic testimony also substantiates this conclusion, as shown in the eight areas above. The early church ascribed Deity to Jesus, especially by calling Him Lord, the Son of God and even God. We also saw that, while the fulness of Deity dwelt in Jesus, He was subordinate to His Father in position. Such is the testimony of both Jesus and the early church. He was fully God, but subordinate to the Father in position. Such a distinction is crucial in order to understand Jesus' own conception and teaching of His Deity and position.

In accordance with our key principle above, we see that God vindicated the full Deity of Christ, including Jesus' subordinate position in the Godhead, by raising Jesus from the dead. We might also state that if Jesus was wrong, especially in this area, it would constitute the supreme example of heresy and God would not have raised Him from the dead. But as God did raise Him, God's stamp of approval thereby demonstrated that Jesus' teachings concerning His Person were valid and accurate.

### God's Approval of Jesus' Other Teachings

We explained above that in raising Jesus from the dead, God placed His stamp of approval on Jesus' entire message. Thus, not only were Jesus' teachings concerning His Person true, but His teachings in other areas were also vindicated.

We saw that there were two major reasons for affirming Jesus' entire message. Positively, we saw that God was acting in accordance with His attributes in raising Jesus from the dead. Several indications of this were given. In so doing, God approved of Jesus' total message, even as Jesus had claimed.

Negatively, God would not have raised a heretic from the dead, since such an act would be contrary to His nature. Therefore, if Jesus' teachings were incorrect pertaining either to His Person or in other areas, God would not have placed His stamp of approval on Jesus' entire message, which He did by raising Jesus.

Thus, if Jesus erred in teaching a doctrine, then He was not speaking God's words at that point. It is noteworthy that the Jewish test of a true spokesman was precisely that He must always speak correctly when delivering God's message. Any incorrect teaching or prophesying called for that person's death as a false prophet. In contrast, God's coming prophet (the Messiah) would speak God's very words (Deut. 18:18-22).

For these reasons, then, we may affirm Jesus' teachings. We have already seen several examples of this. First, Jesus' teachings on His Person were already perceived to be valid.

In dealing with the Deity of Christ, it was also noted that the center of Jesus' preaching was the kingdom of God and its entrance requirements of salvation. Jesus proclaimed that He was the personal agent of God's salvation. Therefore, the entrance requirements of God's kingdom and an individual's eternal destiny rested on how he responded to the Person and salvation message of Jesus Christ. We will deal more extensively with the doctrine of the kingdom of God in Chapter 4 and with the entrance requirements of salvation in Chapter 5. Suffice it to say here that since this twofold topic was the chief message of Jesus, it was especially vindicated and shown to be the truth by Jesus' resurrection.

A related area, and the subject of Appendix 3, concerns

the eternal life of those who respond correctly to the message of Christ. This topic has obvious implications in light of Jesus' resurrection. Since Jesus did rise, the reality of eternal life after death is also valid, as affirmed by the New Testament (II Cor. 4:14; I Thess. 4:14; Rom. 14:9).

A topic of considerable debate today, especially in evangelical circles, concerns the inspiration of the Scriptures. Although it is not always popular to affirm the total trustworthiness and inerrancy of the Scriptures, we will assert in Appendix 2 that such is demanded by Jesus' teachings in this area.

Such are examples of the use of our key principle given in this chapter. As Jesus' entire message has been vindicated by God's raising of Him from the dead, we may trust His teachings concerning both His Person and in other areas.

We may now illustrate the first three steps of our apologetic as follows:

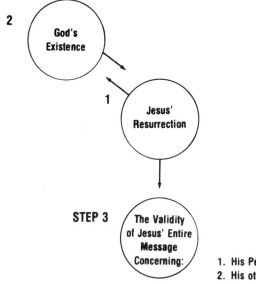

# CHAPTER FOUR

# The Kingdom of God

To summarize our conclusions briefly, we have first seen that the resurrection of Jesus is a literal historical event. Second, we determined that God both exists and was the one who raised Jesus from the dead. Third, we perceived that Jesus' message (concerning both His Person and in other areas of His teaching) is valid. Accordingly, we will turn now to the major emphasis in Jesus' teaching.

## Jesus' Central Teaching

There is little doubt today that Jesus' central message was the kingdom of God and the required response necessary for individual admittance and participation in the blessings of the kingdom. In this chapter we will deal with the concept of the kingdom in Jesus' teaching, turning in the next chapter to the "entrance requirements" in the form of the personal decision required by Jesus.

Contemporary scholars readily admit that the kingdom

of God and the necessary personal salvation response is Jesus' central teaching.[1] Theologians also agree that Jesus taught that the kingdom was an eschatological concept.[2] However, there are differences as to the timing of the kingdom. Various views are offered as to whether Jesus taught that the kingdom was primarily a present or a future reality.[3]

*Consistent eschatology* is often associated with the names of Albert Schweitzer and Johannes Weiss and their work in the late nineteenth and early twentieth centuries. This view stressed the importance of the future apocalyptic in the message of Jesus, who believed that the kingdom would be brought about by a supernatural act of God. Jesus expected that it would arrive soon, yet it was not a present reality in any sense except that Satan was being defeated. Therefore, Jesus had to wait, like everyone else, for the future revelation of God's power.

But for Schweitzer and Weiss, Jesus' view is not authoritative for modern faith. This is both because Jesus is said to be mistaken in His ideas concerning the kingdom and because faith should not be placed in the historical sayings or actions of Jesus.[4]

---

[1]See, for example, Fuller, *The Foundations of New Testament Christology*, pp. 103-106; Rudolf Bultmann, *Jesus Christ and Mythology* (New York: Charles Scribner's Sons, 1958), p. 11; Bultmann, *Theology of the New Testament*, volume I, pp. 4-11; Bornkamm, *Jesus of Nazareth*, pp. 64-95; Wolfhart Pannenberg, *Theology and the Kingdom of God*, edited by Richard John Neuhaus (Philadelphia: The Westminster Press, 1969), p. 51; Brown, *Jesus: God and Man*, pp. 101-104; George E. Ladd, *The Pattern of New Testament Truth* (Grand Rapids: William B. Eerdman's Publishing Company, 1968), p. 61, for instance.

[2]Fuller, Ibid., p. 103; Bultmann, *Jesus Christ and Mythology*, Ibid., p. 13.

[3]For brief surveys of various approaches to the kingdom of God, see Ladd, *The Pattern of New Testament Truth*, pp. 47-63 and Bernard Ramm, *A Handbook of Contemporary Theology* (Grand Rapids: William B. Eerdman's Publishing Company, 1966), pp. 43-45, 78-79.

[4]Schweitzer, *The Quest of the Historical Jesus*, pp. 238-241, 398-403.

The views of Schweitzer and Weiss did show that the kingdom of God was proclaimed by Jesus to be a future act of God. Men could not bring it about by their own power.

However, this view failed to account for several factors. It did not allow for the present aspect of the kingdom. As we saw earlier, Jesus believed that in His Person and message, God was presently confronting man with a decision. Additionally, we have already perceived how Jesus' literal historical resurrection gave the ultimate authority to His message, demonstrating it to be correct. This especially applies to Jesus' teachings on the kingdom of God, since this was His central message. As noted above, it was the content of this message in particular which was verified since Jesus delcared that He did not know the time factor (Mark 13:32). Thus, as we will perceive in the next chapter, faith actually *does* depend on what happened to Jesus in history. In missing these points, Schweitzer and Weiss presented a faulty Christology. Therefore, Jesus was not deluded as to the present or future reality of the kingdom.

A few decades later, Charles Dodd stressed the present kingdom at the expense of its future aspect. His view, known as *realized eschatology,* postulated that there was no future compendium of events yet to occur. In his work *The Parables of the Kingdom,* he popularized the view that the kingdom was not to occur in the near future. Rather, it was already a part of present, realized experience. For Dodd, the kingdom was actually the invasion of the trans-historical into history.[5]

There are some obvious problems with Dodd's view. For instance, he was not taking into account a portion of Jesus' message—that dealing with the kingdom as having its con-

---

[5]Charles H. Dodd, *Parables of the Kingdom* (London: Nisbet and Company, Ltd., 1936), cf. pp. 46-51, 107-108, 197.

summation in the future. Jesus' resurrection verified His teaching about this future aspect of the kingdom as well, just as it guaranteed the validity of the present aspect.

Additionally, Ladd points out that Dodd's position is also faulty in not aligning itself with Scriptural concepts. The Jews did not conceive of the kingdom as a trans-historical reality.[6]

In the *consistent* and *realized* eschatologies, we plainly detect the problems involved in not presenting a view which is balanced by Jesus' teachings concerning both the present and the future reality of the kingdom of God. As both are taught by Jesus, a proper concept of the kingdom should include both.

The future aspect of the kingdom is often obvious in Jesus' message. For instance, He teaches His disciples to pray that God's kingdom will come (Matt. 6:10). At the Last Supper, Jesus asserts that He will not drink of the fruit of the vine until He does so in the future kingdom (Mark 14:25). In Matt. 25:31-46 Jesus speaks of the coming judgment in the last days and the eternal life of the kingdom which will follow. He also describes a series of events which will surround the time of His coming and inaugurate the final revelation of the kingdom (Mark 13; Matt. 24; Luke 21). Jesus also equates the eternal life of the age to come (after the resurrection of the dead) with the kingdom (Mark 9:43-47; 10:23, 30).

There is a sense in which the future kingdom is present, however. Jesus sent His disciples out in order to proclaim that the kingdom was at hand (Matt. 10:7). Jesus also speaks of His casting out demons as a sign that the kingdom had arrived (Luke 11:20). In fact, when questioned by the Pharisees as to when the kingdom would come,

---

[6]See Ladd, *The Pattern of New Testament Truth*, p. 48.

Jesus responded that it was already among them (Luke 17:20, 21).

It is evident that Jesus equated the present inbreaking of the kingdom with His personal ministry and preaching. For instance, we notice that in Luke 11:19 the sons of the Pharisees did not inaugurate the coming of the kingdom when they cast out demons. Rather, it accompanied Jesus' casting them out (v. 20). There was a sense in which Jesus realized that it was His presence that was the deciding factor (Matt. 11:6; 13:16).[7] Therefore, it was in His works and preaching that the kingdom of God was at hand (Mark 1:15).

It is for reasons such as these that contemporary New Testament studies endeavor to work out the relationship between the present and future reality of the kingdom.[8] A few examples will reveal this. According to Bultmann, Jesus conceived of the kingdom as a future, apocalyptic inbreaking into history, which was already erupting into present reality.[9] For Fuller, Jesus taught the proleptic presence of the yet future revelation of God's kingdom. At present the kingdom was hidden, awaiting final consummation.[10]

Bornkamm is also careful to relate the present and future aspects of the kingdom. He asserts that we cannot accept Dodd's *realized eschatology*, but neither can we hold that Jesus taught only a future revelation of God's reign. For Bornkamm, these two aspects cannot be either spiritualized or separated. The present dawning of the kingdom reveals the future salvation and judgment, while the future unlocks the present by presenting it as the day of decision.[11]

---

[7] Fuller, *The Foundations of New Testament Christology*, p. 104.

[8] Cf. Ramm, *A Handbook of Contemporary Theology*, p. 78.

[9] Bultmann, *Theology of the New Testament*, volume I, pp. 4-11.

[10] Fuller, *Foundations of New Testament Christology*, p. 104.

[11] Bornkamm, *Jesus of Nazareth*, especially pp. 90-92.

Ladd's study of this concept is an indepth and especially informative one. Briefly, in Jesus the kingdom was actually present in history, though in a veiled form. The future glorious coming at the end of history will finalize what was already begun in history.[12]

The primary difference between Ladd's view and that of Bultmann, Norman Perrin, and others is that Ladd refuses to demythologize the historic reality of the future coming of the kingdom. Bultmann, for instance, demythologizes the teachings of the apocalyptic kingdom in order to reinterpret it in terms of human existence. For Ladd, such is neither a correct interpretation of the Jewish hope or a fair way to deal with Jesus' own teachings on this subject. The coming of the future manifestation of the kingdom is historical, as was the first coming of Jesus. Thus, it is a relevant reality even for modern man.[13]

It is apparent from our foregoing brief study that contemporary theologians have seen the need to understand *both* the present and future aspects of the kingdom of God. As we concluded above, it is well-recognized in contemporary thought that the present aspect is revealed in the person, works, and message of Jesus. Thus, Jesus confronted men with the kingdom in His works and in His call for decision.[14]

There is also virtual agreement that Jesus conceived of a future manifestation of the kingdom. This consumation was believed by Jesus to be an entering of man's history, characterized by the coming of the Son of man, the resur-

---

[12]Ladd, *The Pattern of New Testament Truth,* especially pp. 61, 63.

[13]For Ladd's criticism of such contemporary demythologizing theologies, see *The Pattern of New Testament Truth,* pp. 49–63, which is a summary of a more indepth criticism contained in his work *Jesus and the Kingdom.*

[14]Bultmann, *Theology of the New Testament,* volume 1, pp. 7–11; Fuller, *The Foundations of New Testament Christology,* pp. 104–106; Bornkamm, *Jesus of Nazareth,* pp. 92–95; Ladd, *The Pattern of New Testament Truth,* pp. 56, 63.

rection of the dead, the conquering and judgment of evil to eternal punishment, and the ushering in of an eternal life of blessedness for those who obeyed Christ's message.[15]

But the key question here, as we have just seen, is whether such claims of Jesus are valid for modern man, or whether they have to be counted as myth and reinterpreted to fit the existential needs of modern man.[16] Ladd's defense of Jesus' concept with regards to demythologization has been noted briefly above.

Applying the principle which we stated earlier, since God raised Jesus from the dead, He placed His stamp of approval on Jesus' teachings on this and every other area. Thus, we have a guarantee that Jesus' concepts concerning both the present and future aspects of the kingdom of God are valid.

---

[15]Bultmann, Ibid., pp. 5-6. It should be noted here that it is the express desire of this author not to deal with the subjects of the rapture and the millennium. Such would take us far off our present course, which is to establish the validity of the general outline of God's kingdom.

[16]It is sometimes asserted that Jesus believed in an immanent kingdom which would culminate very shortly. The support for this view is usually an appeal to Mark 9:1 and 13:30. This objection may be answered along several lines. For instance, incorrect exegesis of these passages is common. Mark 9:1 (cf. Matt. 16:28; Luke 9:27) most likely refers to the transfiguration of Jesus, which follows in each of these narratives, especially since II Peter 1:16-18 uses the same language to refer directly to Jesus' transfiguration. Mark 13:30 states that the generation *then living* in the last days will witness the ushering in of the kingdom. This is evident from verse 32, where Jesus specifically says that He did not even know when He would return. Additionally, this objection is also due to a failure to understand both the present and the future aspects of the kingdom. Lastly, we must remember that Jesus' message, especially in His central teaching concerning the kingdom, was validated by God raising Him from the dead. It is very important to keep in mind that since Jesus specifically declared that even He did not know when the kingdom would come (Mark 13:32), the exact time factor is not the crucial portion of His message. Rather, the *content* concerning the kingdom itself and the entrance requirements of salvation occupies this central position, as pointed out in Chapters IV and V. In other words, God especially validated the content of Jesus' message concerning the kingdom and salvation, not the specific time factor, since Jesus carefully taught that He was not given that knowledge.

Even if many modern men cannot accept such teachings about the future revelation of the kingdom, this does not make them untrue. The literal resurrection of Jesus is also hard for many modern men to accept, yet we have seen that it occurred in real time-space history. Therefore, once again, in light of the historicity of Jesus' resurrection, we perceive that Jesus' teachings concerning the future revelation of God's kingdom are also truth and will literally come to pass in the future. God has assured us of this by His action in this event.

With this assurance, we may now assert the reality of the kingdom as taught by Jesus. The kingdom of God is the entrance of God into human history in order to reign over men. The present aspect of the kingdom was inaugurated by Jesus. In this "hidden" form it was represented by Jesus' works and teaching, confronting man with a decision to accept the reign of God by accepting Jesus' person and His salvation message. The future form of the kingdom will enter history on a wider scale, characterized by Jesus' return to earth, the resurrection of the dead, and judgment. Subsequently, those who refused the reign of God will be banished to eternal punishment. Those who accepted God's reign through Christ's message will be rewarded with an eternal life of blessedness in a body like Christ's resurrected body.[17]

## God's Confirmation

We have dealt in this chapter with Jesus' teaching concerning the kingdom of God, in both its present and future aspects. We concluded by stressing God's acceptance and verification of this message by raising Jesus from the

---

[17]See Ladd, *The Pattern of New Testament Truth*, p. 63.

dead. A final word will be directed here to the certainty of that approval.

We have shown that the center of Jesus' teaching was confronting men with the kingdom of God and the message of its entrance requirements of salvation. That this was the major emphasis of Jesus' teachings is a very important point here, because it reveals the area concerning which we may know that God approved. This certainly does not mean to imply that God did not approve all of Jesus' other teachings, since this aspect has been supported above several times. However, the point being made here is that since the kingdom and the corresponding message of salvation occupied the central position in Jesus' teachings, it can be accepted as the direct word of God to men. Thus, by raising Jesus, God would especially be emphasizing Jesus' chief message, since He would not have raised a heretic from the dead.

Therefore, this message of the kingdom demands the utmost respect. It is not a doctrine to be taken lightly because it is contrary to the feelings of contemporary man. Jesus' message of the kingdom demands a response from the individual, as we will see more clearly in the next chapter. Especially since the kingdom is the center of Jesus' message, we know that God approved of it. In short, those who refuse Jesus' message are doing so contrary to God's strongest approval.

The chart on page 100 will illustrate the four major points of our apologetic which we have made thus far.

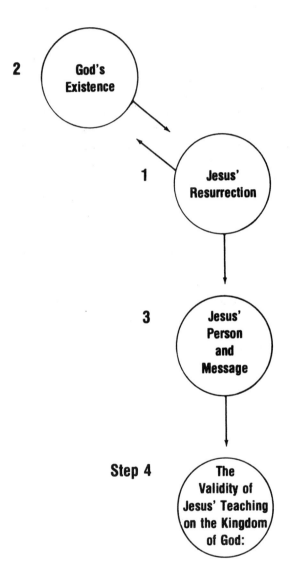

# CHAPTER FIVE

# Salvation

To review briefly, we have shown, first, that Jesus' resurrection literally occurred in history. Second, we perceived that God both exists and that He did perform this event. Third, in so doing, God approved and vindicated Jesus' entire message concerning both His Person and other teachings.

Next, we ascertained that the central message of Jesus was confronting men with a decision concerning the kingdom of God. In the fourth chapter we dealt with the actual concept of the kingdom, showing that Jesus' teaching concerning both its present and future aspects is valid.

## Jesus' Central Teaching

In this fifth chapter we will examine the remaining portion of Jesus' central teaching. Having studied the actual concept of the kingdom of God in the last chapter, we will turn now to the personal decision (the "entrance requirements") which Jesus asserted was necessary for admittance to and participation in the blessings of eternal life in the kingdom.

Even among contemporary critical scholars themselves, we find a general agreement with regards to the content of Jesus' teachings concerning the salvation message. Most twentieth-century theologians admit the reality of sin to varying degrees. They also realize that an important part of Jesus' message was concerned with the reality of sin and its remedy.[1] Jesus believed that He was sent to proclaim the answer to this dilemma. This solution consisted of the culmination of His mission, which was His own death for the sins of the world. From Jesus Himself this message also became the center of New Testament Christology.[2]

In light of these truths, Jesus confronted men with a decision. He preached the necessity of repentance from sin,[3] which involved a complete change of life from old habits. He additionally proclaimed the need for an exercise of faith in God and in His own Person and message. Thus, men were to believe in Him as God's chosen messenger and to exercise obedience to His offer of forgiveness in light of the future judgment.[4]

---

[1] See Bultmann, *Theology of the New Testament,* volume I, pp. 21-22; Barth, *Church Dogmatics,* volume IV, Part I, pp. 252-256, 358, for instance; Emil Brunner, *Dogmatics* (Three volumes; Philadelphia: The Westminster Press, 1952), volume II, *The Christian Doctrine of Creation and Redemption,* pp. 89ff; cf. Ramm, *A Handbook of Contemporary Theology,* pp. 117-119.

[2] See Vincent Taylor, *The Atonement in New Testament Teaching* (Third edition; London: The Epworth Press, 1963), p. 5; Vincent Taylor, *The Gospel According to St. Mark* (London: Macmillan and Co., Ltd. 1963), pp. 445-446; Barth, Ibid., pp. 211ff., especially pp. 251-256; Brunner, Ibid., pp. 249, 281ff.; Cullmann, *The Christology of the New Testament,* pp. 65, 110; Ramm, Ibid., pp. 16-17.

[3] Bultmann, *Theology of the New Testament,* volume I, pp. 20-21; Marxsen, *The Resurrection of Jesus of Nazareth,* p. 169.

[4] Cf. Brunner, *Dogmatics,* volume II, pp. 298-305; Brown, *Jesus: God and Man,* pp. 96-99, 101; Barth, *Church Dogmatics,* volume IV, part I, pp. 248-251; Fuller, *The Foundations of New Testament Christology,* pp. 105-106; Bultmann, "New Testament and Mythology", p. 22; Bornkamm, *Jesus of Nazareth,* pp. 92-94; Ramm, *A Handbook of Contemporary Theology,* pp. 30-31, 48-49.

Concerning this last point, Emil Brunner has made some noteworthy comments. Brunner points out that if Jesus had only come proclaiming the kingdom and the need of men to respond in obedience in order to share in its benefits, then He would only have been one of the prophets. But Jesus did more than this, for He confronted men with the decision to accept His Person and message by faith, as the very means of participation in the kingdom.[5]

In a similar respect, Raymond Brown relates that the *historical minimum* in the words of Jesus is that He proclaimed that in His preaching, deeds, and in His own Person, He was God's unique presentation of the kingdom message. God's rule over men was established through Him, by belief in Him, and by the accompanying commitment.[6]

Before examining the New Testament record of Jesus' teaching on salvation, it is important to repeat an important distinction made earlier concerning the evaluation of the plan of salvation by critical theologians. Our brief survey here does show that there is general agreement on Jesus' teachings on this subject. However, it cannot be stressed enough that often there is a significant difference between definitions of the words used here. For instance, a good example is the concept of sin. Contemporary theologians generally agree that man is sinful, but usually as an existential state and not based on the time-space, historical fall of Adam. Another example concerns the atonement, which is often defined differently than Jesus or the New Testament defined this word, perhaps by ignoring the concept of the blood sacrifice or Jesus' substitutionary death.[7] Such distinctions are crucial before proceeding to Jesus' teachings.

---

[5] Brunner, Ibid.
[6] Brown, *Jesus: God and Man*, pp. 96-99, 101.
[7] Ramm, *A Handbook of Contemporary Theology*, cf. pp. 8-9, 16-18, 117-119.

Thus, critical scholars often reject Jesus' literal teachings while sometimes holding to the general concept behind them. But since the resurrection has been shown to be a literal historical event, contemporary theologians face a dilemma at this point. No longer should Jesus' Deity or atonement, for example, be literally rejected or spiritualized based on the belief that Jesus did not literally rise from the dead. Since Jesus' teachings rely on the resurrection, which is well recognized by almost all scholars, these teachings should be literally accepted since the event also occurred literally. Thus, the general agreement by critical scholars noted above should most logically become literal agreement in view of the facts.

With this distinction in mind, we proceed now to Jesus' teachings on salvation. We are careful to note that God vindicated Jesus' literal message of salvation, especially since it was His central teaching.

According to Jesus' own teaching, all men are sinners and forgiveness of these sins is necessary (Luke 24:47; Mark 8:38). With men this is impossible (Matt. 19:25-26). Jesus claimed that the provision for this salvation would therefore be made by His substitutionary death and shed blood for the sins of the world (Mark 10:45; Matt. 26:28), as well as by His resurrection from the dead (Luke 24:45-47). As a result, Jesus called for repentance (Luke 13:1-5) and faith in His Person and message as the means of entrance into the kingdom of God and the obtaining of eternal life (Mark 1:15; Luke 24:47; John 6:47). The result was a changed life of total commitment (Luke 14:25-35).

From Jesus, the early church also proclaimed the message that all had sinned (Rom. 3:10-12, 23; I John 1:8, 10) and so God made a remedy for sin by sending Christ (Rom. 6:23). Jesus died a subsititutionary death for these sins (I Cor. 15:3; Rom. 5:8), His shed blood being the means of forgiveness (Eph. 1:7; I Peter 1:18, 19; Heb.

9:12-14). Then He rose from the dead to complete this provision for salvation (Rom. 10:9; I Cor. 15:3, 4). Man could not gain this salvation by his own good works or in his own power (Eph. 2:8-10). Therefore, repentance (Acts 2:38; 3:19) and faith in Christ and His work were required for salvation (Acts 16:31; 13:38, 39; Rom. 10:9). A new life of commitment and obedience resulted (II Cor. 5:17-18; I John 2:3-5).

In the messages of Christ and the early church, two concepts in particular deserve brief explanations. First, "repentance" was not taken to be merely a remorse for sin, as it is often used today in English. Rather, the Greek word (μετανοέω) denotes a complete change of mind. Such a change is almost always spoken of as the renouncing of sin and living a life of commitment to God.[8] Second, "belief" or "faith" was a very strong word compared to its counterpart in English, where it is often used simply to express agreement. The Greek word (πιστεύω) signifies being persuaded to the extent of placing one's confidence, reliance, or trust in someone or something. As used with regards to Jesus, it involves commitment and surrender to His Person and message.[9]

As we saw in Chapter 4, compliance with Jesus' message gained admittance to the kingdom of God and participation in eternal life. In Jesus' message, we see references to the eternal life of the kingdom and the blessings for the faithful.[10] From Jesus, the early church also taught the blessings of eternal life.[11] This is the result of a positive

---

[8]Vine, *An Expository Dictionary of New Testament Words*, volume III, pp. 279-280.
[9]Ibid., volume I, pp. 116-117, 211.
[10]See, for example, Mark 9:43-47; 12:25; Matt. 6:19-20; 7:13-14; 8:11; Luke 12:33; 16:19-31. Cf. Bultmann, *Theology of the New Testament*, volume I, pp. 5-6.
[11]See I Cor. 2:9, 15:50-53; II Cor. 5:1-9; Rev. 21-22 for examples. Cf. Rudolf Bultmann, *History and Eschatology: The Presence of Eternity* (New York: Harper and Row, Publishers, 1957), pp. 32-33.

decision of accepting Jesus' message and responding in faith and commitment.

## God's Confirmation

We have briefly studied Jesus' message of salvation and have seen that He believed that certain personal requirements were necessary for entering God's kingdom. Because all men are sinners and cannot relieve this condition themselves by good works or otherwise, Jesus stated that He came to die and shed His blood to pay for this sin. This act of salvation was culminated in His resurrection from the dead. Therefore, repentance was demanded in the sense of turning from one's sin and turning to God by faith in Christ. This belief, as we saw above, signified trusting Jesus' death as a payment for personal sin and being committed to His Person and message of salvation. The results of this repentance and acceptance of Jesus included a changed life brought about by the indwelling Holy Spirit and eternal life in God's kingdom.

This view of the gospel, taught by both Jesus and the early church, is often considered to be outdated today. But several facts have shown both that Jesus' message, especially in this area, is valid and that it is equally binding on men today.

One of the major themes in this book has been that, in raising Jesus from the dead, God approved of Jesus' entire message. Two corollaries of this truth have a bearing on the issue being raised here. The first concerns the literal resurrection; the second concerns Jesus' central teaching of salvation and entrance into the kingdom of God.

First, contemporary theologians admit these teachings to have been the view of both Jesus and the early church, but they often do not grant them literal truthfulness, especially for modern man. It is often true that a literal resurrection is not accepted either.

However, since Jesus *literally* rose from the dead, as already demonstrated in Chapter 1, it is our assertion that the teachings of Jesus should also be accepted *literally*. To repeat, the teachings were often refused literal adherence because the event on which they were based was also affirmed in a nonliteral way. However, with the foundation for the literal resurrection found to be firm, so is the foundation for the literal teachings of Jesus. Thus, the event assures the teachings.

Second, in speaking of Jesus' message being approved by God, we are of course speaking of Jesus' concept of salvation as part of that message. But in an important sense, God approved Jesus' presentation of the gospel in particular by raising Him from the dead.

Since the kingdom of God and its entrance requirements are the center of Jesus' teachings, they can be taken most of all as God's message to men. In other words, Jesus was speaking directly for God on this issue of salvation. In raising Jesus, God would especially be emphasizing Jesus' chief message. This is especially evident in the fact that Jesus taught that the major reason He came was to proclaim salvation to men (Mark 2:17; 10:45). We saw earlier that God would not have raised a heretic from the dead.

Raymond Brown offers some pertinent comments on this issue. He points out that Jesus taught the need of faith in Himself and His message in light of the coming kingdom. As Jesus' authority was especially evident in speaking concerning the kingdom, we may assert that He spoke God's will on this issue. And since He spoke God's will it follows that His message is true for every century. No age, modern or otherwise, can reject Jesus' demands as outdated because they are God's words. Thus, belief in Jesus is always needed for salvation.[12]

We therefore find a strong basis for affirming Jesus' message of salvation. Some may doubt its validity today, but, as we saw, God gave the strongest confirmation of it as Jesus' central teaching by raising Him from the dead.

## The Significance of the Substitutionary Blood Atonement of Jesus

We will turn now to two problems which often appear to be major obstacles in a modern acceptance of the plan of salvation as presented in the New Testament. The first of these concerns the concept of Christ dying a substitutionary death and shedding His blood for the sins of man. Especially in modern times this belief has been assailed by critics and even minimized by evangelicals. Yet, as just pointed out above, it is an indispensable part of the salvation message of Jesus.

Even so, the atonement is defended by a number of contemporary scholars, of which only a few may be mentioned here. For instance, Karl Barth's *Church Dogmatics* includes a large amount of material on this subject. For Barth, the key to the atonement is in the overcoming of man's sin, which is best characterized by man's rebellion against God. Jesus, as the very Son of God, died in order to take our place (but not to satisfy God's wrath, Barth explains). By means of Christ's suffering and shed blood, our penalty for sin was removed by faith in Jesus Christ.[13]

In spite of these emphases in Barth's work, there is

---

[12]Brown, *Jesus: God and Man,* p. 101.
[13]Barth, *Church Dogmatics,* volume IV, part I, pp. 211-283, cf. especially pp. 248-254.

another element which is somewhat negative. Barth's theology strongly implies universal salvation for all men in that Christ bore the penalty for everyone, although Barth seemed to resist this conclusion.[14] However, universalism is not compatible with Jesus' exclusive message that salvation is found only in Himself by means of a personal decision. It has been shown how this message was validated by Jesus' resurrection, thus disproving any kind of universalism.

In an essay entitled "The Nature of Redemption," Roger Nicole gives a treatment of the New Testament concept of atonement, after which he evaluates several other theories of the atonement and exposes their weaknesses. For Nicole, the atonement is the center of the Christian faith and the center of the atonement is the substitutionary death of Christ.[15]

One of the strongest defenses of the concept of the atonement from among critical scholars comes from Emil Brunner. He presents his view by addressing himself to a number of questions.

Is the idea of the atonement pre-Christian? Brunner answers that this objection does not come from careful Biblical and theological reasoning, but from rationalistic presuppositions in the thoughts of scholars from Abelard to Fichte. Additionally, Brunner argues, who could label Paul as being "pre-Christian" or "ritualistic"? This certainly does not fit if judged according to his writings. Also, the idea of God sending His Son to die for our sins is anything but primitive. Lastly, Brunner charges that those

[14]See Brunner's *Dogmatics,* volume I, *The Christian Doctrine of God,* pp. 346-353, where Brunner disagrees with Barth's position; cf. Ramm, *A Handbook of Contemporary Theology,* pp. 134-135.
[15]See Nicole's essay "The Nature of Redemption" in *Christian Faith and Modern Theology,* edited by Carl F. H. Henry (New York: Channel Press, 1964), pp. 191-222.

who raise this objection have already decided against the atonement. They do not want to admit its validity because they would rather believe that they can gain forgiveness by themselves.[16]

Why, then, must there have been an atonement? Here Brunner is at his best. First, there must have been a real atonement because sin is real. Here is the crux of the matter. That we have sinned is a fact. Therefore, the removal of the sin must be just as real and necessitates the atonement.

Second, those who reject the idea of atonement gloss over the idea of guilt. It is because they play this aspect down that they cannot understand God's act to forgive that guilt.

Third, there can be a removal of guilt only if God does it. No other means is possible, and God's way is by the atoning death of His Son.[17]

Brunner also asserts that man cannot even ask about the possibility of salvation apart from the atonement. This belief is an *a posteriori* result of God's act in real history, namely, the cross of Christ. This is the only way to real fellowship with God.

However, it is lamentable that even though Brunner stresses the sinful condition of man and the corresponding importance of faith in order to appropriate the results of the atonement, he does appear to spend comparatively little time on the idea of substitution.[18]

James Denney also stresses the importance of Divine necessity in the atonement. God must act consistently on the matter of sin and must also do justice to Himself with regards to it. Since He declared the validity of atonement,

---

[16]Brunner, *Dogmatics,* volume II, pp. 292-294.
[17]Ibid., p. 291.
[18]Ibid., pp. 293-297.

and God cannot deny Himself, it is the only way for forgiveness. Thus, there can be no salvation apart from it. The atonement is therefore an *a posteriori* conclusion based on this knowledge of God's Character.[19]

We may glean at least three strong defenses of the atonement from Brunner and Denney. First, it is an important point that the reality of sin demands a real remedy, even if it costs something. The literalness of the atonement is demanded by the literalness of the sin. An imaginative concept could not forgive a real entity.

Second, the concept of Divine necessity is also crucial. As God has ordained this as the means of forgiveness, He must act consistently. He has declared that this is the only means of forgiveness. Why are we to question Him? At this point we see how the query of finding another way to save men is fruitless, since God declared that this is the only way.

Third, as indicated by Brunner, it is due to rationalism and idealism that the atonement is rejected by many. Thus, many critics of this concept object because of *a priori* philosophical reasoning.

In addition to these reasons, we gave our final defense of the atonement earlier. Jesus declared the truthfulness of the atonement and taught that He came in order to die a substitutionary death by shedding His blood for man's sins. When God raised Him from the dead, He validated these teachings as agreeing with His own will. Thus, while many respond negatively to the idea of an innocent man dying for the sins of others, we should realize that God sent His Son, not another man, to die for us. This was the message of both Christ and the early church, and it was confirmed by God in the resurrection.

---

[19]James Denney, *The Death of Christ,* edited by R. V. G. Tasker (London: The Tyndale Press, 1951), especially pp. 187ff.

Thus we can accept Jesus' teaching concerning His remedy for sin. He did indeed die for mankind. By our repentance and by faith in His Person and message, including trusting His atoning death for us, we may be forgiven of our sins and thereby gain entrance to the eternal life of the kingdom of God.

### A Word Concerning Eternal Punishment

A second major obstacle for many in accepting the gospel concerns the question of eternal punishment. We will address ourselves only briefly to this question, looking at two aspects which argue for its reality.

First, the punishment of the wicked is also a part of Jesus' teaching, where it is often contrasted with the teaching of eternal life for the believer (Mark 9:43-50; Matt. 10:28; Luke 13:24-28).[20] Therefore, it occupies an opposite relationship to Jesus' message concerning the kingdom of God. Just as those who respond correctly to Jesus' call for decision receive an eternal life of blessedness, those who do not do so are judged accordingly. Jesus realized that the majority would reject His word (Matt. 7:13, 14).

Using the principle we established above, God approved Jesus' teachings by raising Him from the dead. In this case, God is approving a teaching which is the other side of Jesus' key teaching concerning entrance into the kingdom. We are therefore on good grounds by accepting its truthfulness.

Second, a real program of punishment would be consistent with the attributes of a good, loving, and perfect God.

---

[20]See also Matt. 5:22, 8:11-12; 13:41-42; Luke 16:19-31. For Bultmann's recognition of this element in the teachings of Jesus, see his *Theology of the New Testament*, volume I, pp. 5-6.

Both philosophically and theologically, God's nature demands such punishment. We can rest assured that God gives men many chances to show whether they will follow Him or not. But when they refuse, there is no alternative. Disobedience cannot go unpunished if God is to be true to His nature.

We must also face the fact that many men will never follow God's ways, even given an infinite amount of chances. Rather than deny a man free will, God gives him that choice to rebel. Geisler states it this way:

> God will permit a man the free choice to do his "thing" eternally, just as He will permit other men to do His "thing" forever. Only those persons will be permitted in heaven who God knows would never change their will; and only those will be pronounced reprobate and eternally "dead" who God knows will never change their will. In brief, the omniscience of God guarantees that the decisions are eternal (cf. Luke 16:26; Heb. 9:27).[21]

Accordingly, some men do choose to rebel against God in this life. As with such afflictions as drug addiction or alcoholism, the person may not *want* such an alternative, but they *will* it nonetheless. Similarly, many may not want the conditions of eternal punishment, but they would never will to follow God's way and be obedient to Him, either. Eternal punishment is thus a final decision, but also a freely made decision.

Therefore, in agreement with the attributes of God, the only way to grant eternal life in the kingdom is to separate sin eternally. Once again, such a choice may not be what the rebellious desire, but it is still what they have willingly chosen.[22]

---

[21]Geisler, *Philosophy of Religion,* especially p. 374.
[22]Ibid., pp. 374–375.

For this reason, then, we can perceive the need for eternal punishment. Men have chances not to rebel, but in their own free will they choose not to follow God. The crux of the matter is that even if the situation could be otherwise, many would not will it so.

Therefore, we see that eternal punishment is warranted according to the evidence. God confirmed Jesus' message of eternal life and eternal punishment by raising Him from the dead. Additionally, such punishment is consistent with God's nature. Here we saw that many even choose such consequences rather than following God.

## Total Commitment

On the subject of total commitment, most contemporary critical theologians have followed the teachings of Søren Kierkegaard. Breaking strongly with the current conception of faith in his day, Kierkegaard (1813–1855) taught that faith was not the mere agreement with a creed, but a radically changed life based on total obedience to God.[23]

In *Attack Upon "Christendom,"* Kierkegaard developed an especially trenchant criticism of those who believed that they could become Christians by intellectual assent apart from a commitment of themselves. In this regard he especially rejected the view of Christianity found in his own country of Denmark, where it was commonly believed that by being a good Danish citizen one would also be a good Christian.[24]

Kierkegaard pointed out that Christianity involved total commitment by following Christ. It cost something to be a

[23]Ramm, *A Handbook of Contemporary Theology*, pp. 48–49.
[24]Søren Kierkegaard, *Attack Upon "Christendom"*, translated by Walter Lowrie (Princeton: Princeton University Press, 1968), pp. 132–133; 164–165.

Christian. Often it involved suffering for one's personal stand. At any rate, a true Christian was one who was surrendered and committed to the teachings of Jesus Christ.[25]

As already stated, most critical scholars followed Kierkegaard in his stress on the cost of living a true Christian life by total commitment. For instance, Bultmann notes that the New Testament view of faith involves obedience and a detachment from the things of this world.[26] This was likewise the message of Jesus, who demanded that men make a choice between God's reign and earthly, material possessions. Jesus called for placing the things of God above riches and even above one's family.[27]

Bornkamm also stresses the call for commitment to true discipleship. Such a commitment to follow Jesus signified one's own determination to abandon all things. This decision demanded the utmost obedience.[28]

It is probable that Dietrich Bonhoeffer was influenced by Kierkegaard's concept of faith more than any other contemporary theologian. Bonhoeffer's well-known work *The Cost of Discipleship* is a stern rebuke to those whose Christianity costs them nothing. Real faith costs something. As asserted by Bonhoeffer, "The call to follow implies that there is only one way of believing on Jesus Christ, and that is by leaving all and going with the incarnate Son of God."[29]

For Bonhoeffer, faith was obedience. In this he was adamant. Faith involved a response from the total person.

---

[25]Ibid., pp. 117–124 gives an example of what is a reoccurring theme in this book.

[26]Bultmann, "New Testament and Mythology", p. 22.

[27]Bultmann, *The Theology of the New Testament,* volume I, pp. 9–11.

[28]Bornkamm, *Jesus of Nazareth,* pp. 144–152.

[29]Dietrich Bonhoeffer, *The Cost of Discipleship,* translated by R. H. Fuller (New York: The Macmillan Company, 1959), p. 67.

It was a wholehearted following of Jesus. Bonhoeffer was also much influenced by Kierkegaard in his concept that the Christian will suffer for his faith. In an often-quoted assertion, Bonhoeffer claimed that "When Christ calls a man, he bids him come and die."[30]

These examples suffice to show some of the influence of Kierkegaard's concept of total commitment. Its strength lies in its comprehension of Christ's call to unreserved obedience on the part of the believer.

Weaknesses in such views can arise in at least two areas. First, many contemporary theologians have properly stressed the call to discipleship, but have made the mistake of calling for a self-surrender to a non-biblical Christ. As was pointed out earlier, New Testament commitment is to a Divine Christ as well as to His message. Without this understanding of Christ as Deity, the concept of commitment is far from complete. Second, as presented by Kierkegaard, faith involves a "leap." It is engaged in apart from rational evidences and even in spite of them. Such is also an incorrect view. As we have also seen above, God's acts in history, such as in Jesus' resurrection, are the foundation for New Testament faith.[31]

With these two qualifications of a Divine Christ and an historical, evidential basis for our faith, we should, indeed, embrace total commitment to God through the Lord Jesus Christ. Jesus proclaimed such a message often.

For instance, Luke 14:25-35 gives three areas in which Christ claimed that He was to be placed first. We must love Christ before our own families and loved ones (vv. 25-26;

---

[30]Ibid., p. 99; see especially pp. 45-104 for these views.

[31]For an examination and critique of Kierkegaard's concept of the leap of faith, see Habermas, *The Resurrection of Jesus: A Rational Inquiry*, pp. 172-197. See pp. 198-224 for a critique of contemporary critical scholars who have followed Kierkegaard in this concept.

cf. Matt. 10:37), before our own lives (vv. 26, 27; cf. Matt. 10:38-39; 16:24-26) and before our possessions (v. 33; cf. Luke 12:33; Matt. 13:44-45). Surely all these things are dear to us, but the call of Christ is to love Him more. In other words, "Seek ye first the kingdom of God and His righteousness" (Matt. 6:33). Such is our priority as believers.

Such a commitment, as we have just seen, begins by placing God first in our lives. All other people and possessions, including ourselves, are subordinate. Such commitment also entails our spending time with God in His Word and in worship and prayer. Our commitment additionally involves fellowship with and love of others. We should share the message of Christ, as well as our time and means with others (cf. Luke 10:25-37).

Our total commitment to God involves the use of our time, talents and possessions. All is subordinate to Him.

We have certainly touched on important matters here. Yet total commitment is certainly taught by Christ and by other New Testament authors. Those who have followed Jesus in repentance and faith are called to submit totally to Him. Such commitment, especially of our time and finances, is a personal matter between ourselves and God and should be worked out in dependence on God and by openness to His leading. Certainly the desire of a true disciple is to be a good steward of what God has given him, thus using as little as possible with regards to himself and as much as possible for God's work.[32]

---

[32]For some very good and thought provoking discussions of total commitment, see Bonhoeffer, *The Cost of Discipleship,* George Verwer, *Come! Live! Die!: The Real Revolution* (Wheaton: Tyndale House Publishers, 1972); William Mac-Donald, *True Discipleship* (Walterick Publishers, Box 2216, Kansas City, Kansas); David Gill, "Radical Christian: Rethinking Our Financial Priorities" in *Right On,* volume 7, number 6, February-March (1976): p. 12 (Box 4307, Berkeley, California, 94704).

## Conclusion

In this chapter we concluded that all men are sinners and that Jesus died a substitutionary death, shedding His blood for the sins of mankind. His resurrection completed this provision for sin. Entrance into the kingdom of God depends on one's repentance from sin and faith (in the sense of real trust) in the Person and work of Christ on our behalf. Such a view is demanded by God's verification of this message of Jesus by raising Him from the dead. This message is additionally corroborated in that it was Jesus' central teaching, thus meaning that God especially approved it.

We additionally found that this concept of the atonement is a valid view. Such is required both by man's real sinfulness and by the nature of God, who provided this one way of salvation. Divine necessity requires that God be consistent with His own proclamation. By raising Jesus from the dead, the truth of Jesus' teachings about His atoning death was also corroborated.

Eternal punishment is also demanded by the nature of God. Sin must be eternally separated from righteousness. God knows who would refuse His offer of salvation no matter how many times it was offered. Although the option of eternal punishment is not a desirable one, many do choose it, nonetheless, by their denial of God. God additionally showed His acceptance of this teaching by raising Jesus, thus confirming His testimony as to its truthfulness.

Lastly, total commitment is a challenge to all believers. Jesus bid us to place God above our family, self and possessions. We should endeavor to work out such a total self-surrender in accordance with God's leading in our lives.

We will now illustrate our apologetic as follows:

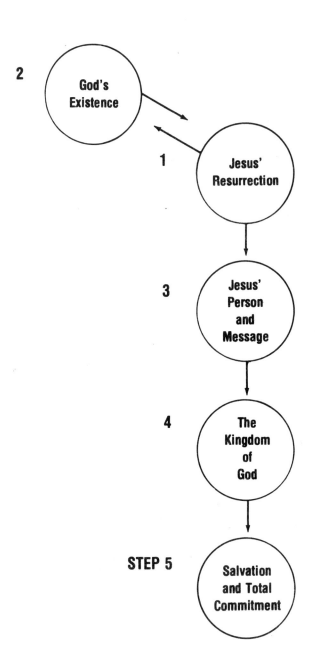

# Part Two

An Expansion and Explication
of Several Inclusive Topics

# The Resurrection and World Views

We have now concluded our first five chapters encompassing the major presentation of our apologetic system based on the resurrection. We first demonstrated the historicity of Jesus' resurrection. Second, we established the fact that God both exists and performed this event. Third, in raising Jesus, we showed that God approved Jesus' entire message, pertaining both to Jesus' Person and to His other teachings.

We then studied Jesus' central teaching, in particular concerning the kingdom of God and the entrance requirements of salvation. We asserted, fourth, the validity of Jesus' concept of the kingdom. Fifth, we investigated Jesus' teaching concerning personal salvation being the only way to enter the kingdom and found that this message was especially valid in light of His resurrection.

We will turn now in the appendices to several areas of interest which either expand points which we have already made or which explicate related ramifications of the above apologetic. In this chapter we will examine various other world views in light of Jesus' resurrection. It should be noted that we are not dealing with the entire philosophy of these other positions, as this would take us much beyond the scope of this appendix. Rather, we will be examining these views in relation to selected points of Christian theology.

## A Key Principle

Throughout this book, the historicity of the resurrection has been the pivotal point of discussion. We have shown both that this event literally occurred and that it provides the center for Christian theology in general and for apologetics in particular. As such, we have perceived that it is not an isolated event which should simply be ignored. Rather, many truths are dependent upon its reality.

In Chapter 2 it was shown that a theistic universe could be established by theistic argumentation. It was then pointed out how the resurrection of Jesus could answer the question of *which* theistic world view was correct, since this historical event firmly establishes the Christian world view. In a second and independent argument, we also showed how it was valid to reason from a combination of Jesus' resurrection and His claims concerning His Person and message back to His theistic world view, which is the same Christian world view established by the first argument.

Accordingly, since the resurrection actually occurred and Christian theism is therefore correct by virtue of our prospective and retrospective arguments stated above, certain theological and historical beliefs are thus valid and other such beliefs are not. Here we have a criterion of truth, especially in such disciplines as theology and philosophy, with which we may evaluate other world views.

Because of this, we may now state a general principle which will guide us in this appendix. Since our two arguments above show that Christian theism is therefore valid, we may conclude that theological and philosophical world views, in particular, must align their beliefs with this position. In other words, *such world views must bring their own systems into accordance with the facticity of the resurrection and subsequent Christian theism in order to be factual themselves.* Thus, if the resurrection and corresponding Christian world view corrects or establishes a concept, it must be accepted or the opposing view will be in error at that point.

This criterion will be employed in our evaluation of several major world views which are contrary to Christianity. As shown earlier, the resurrection validates the truthfulness of various doctrines. This guideline can therefore be utilized as a critique of opposing positions with regard to these doctrines.

## A Refutation of World Views

We will turn now to a presentation of several key areas of theology. It is our desire to examine several examples of contemporary approaches to each of these doctrines in order to contrast these views with the interpretation which is demanded by the literal resurrection of Jesus and His Christian world view.[1]

---

[1]Again, we do not desire to indiscriminately separate the resurrection of Jesus from other apologetic evidences. Therefore, it should be noted here that fulfilled prophecy, for instance, is also a very useful evidence in determining that the Christian world view is the best theism.

## God

Naturalistic schools of thought,[2] by definition, hold that this universe is explicable in terms of its own existence. There is no need to resort to supernatural explanations such as God's creation, intervention, or sustaining power. Rather, natural processes are capable of giving rise to and operating the system.

As just pointed out above, our twofold argument in Chapter 2 provides two independent validations of the Christian theistic world view. Our first study concerning several valid theistic arguments is a most obvious refutation here, as some of the attributes of God were revealed, including the creation and sustaining of the universe. This further points out that the universe is not a valid explanation of its own existence.

Our second study concerning a combination of the literal resurrection plus Jesus' claims also shows that God both exists and that He intervened into nature to perform this event. This twofold argument thereby disproves naturalisms.

In Chapter 2 we also showed how both logical positivism and linguistic analysis fall prey to such criticisms as well. Other naturalisms are likewise faulty in not postulating God's existence and activity in the universe. Atheism and God-is-dead theology are most obviously in error in light of this data, since God both exists and is active. Agnosticism is also incorrect, for we can indeed gain limited knowledge concerning God in light of the foregoing analysis.

---

[2]Schools of thought are obviously made up of individual scholars and thus there are often exceptions to characterizing an entire group by one title. Speaking generally, however, when referring to naturalistic views, we are speaking of such movements as positivism, linguistic analysis, philosophical existentialism, pragmatism, at least as modified by John Dewey, Marxism and atheism.

Idealistic schools of thought[3] hold that the ideal or spiritual world is the real and most important world, thus offering an alternative to naturalism. God is often spoken of by idealists as Mind or Spirit and is generally considered to be more or less immanent in the world process.[4]

Contrary to immanental philosophies and liberal theologies, theistic argumentation[5] and the coupling of Jesus' resurrection with His claims provides two arguments which show that God is transcendent, working in nature from outside of it by temporarily suspending the laws of nature, as pointed out especially in Chapter II. Thus, nature must look beyond itself in order to explain its own existence.

Naturalistic systems and idealistic views both agree that God does not perform miracles. He simply does not interfere with nature in order to act. Critical theology as a whole confirms this opinion. Process philosophy (or panentheism), whereby God is hypothesized as being both transcendent (potentially) and immanent (actually), also agrees against the existence of miracles. We might say that non-biblical philosophical systems as a whole accept this judgment.

However, the resurrection combined with Jesus' teachings shows most emphatically that God does act miracu-

---

[3]Generally speaking, we are identifying Platonism, neo-Platonism, panpsychism, subjective idealism, absolute idealism, personalism, and theological liberalism as various movements within idealism.

[4]In idealistic systems, God is usually immanent, or at least partially so. For instance, various forms of pantheism conceive of God as being identical with the whole of reality, in which case individual things are actually particulars of His own existence. Neo-Platonists believed that this world was an "overflow" of divine essence. For Leibniz, reality is made up of metaphysical units called monads, of which God is the highest "Monad of Monads". Hegel's Absolute Spirit is the process itself, progressing by means of the dialectic process. Theological liberalism is an especially good example of an immanental philosophy.

[5]See Geisler, *Philosophy of Religion*, pp. 215-218.

lously in nature.[6] By exercising a superior power, He intervened in nature to raise Jesus from the dead. This gives us a firm ground, on the one hand, to accept other biblical accounts of miracles as being both possible and actual. On the other hand, it gives us another strong refutation of philosophies which deny such events.

It is true that some idealisms conceive of God in personal terms. Yet non-biblical philosophical and theological schools of thought also agree that God was never actually incarnated, as Scripture claims. But we have already seen that Christ was God and yet took the form of man. Jesus' resurrection shows that His teaching concerning His own Deity was true.

We may briefly summarize by stating that in studying belief in God, theistic argumentation and the resurrection coupled with Jesus' claims concerning His Person and message provide two valid arguments for concluding that a scriptural philosophy is the correct one. Both of these arguments verify God's existence and actions, thereby showing that all naturalistic world views are incorrect.

On the other hand, both arguments also reveal that God is transcendent, working in nature from outside of it. This disproves the idealistic philosophies and theologies, which generally claim that God is immanent. The historicity of the resurrection plus Jesus' claims also invalidate both naturalistic and idealistic philosophies which hold that such miracles do not occur. In addition, God's revelation in the Person of Jesus Christ also disproves non-biblical philosophies and theologies which disclaim such a personal revelation of God to man. We therefore perceive that both of our arguments have shown that the biblical view of God is the correct view.

---

[6]Again, prophecy also helps to establish the fact that God works in nature, bringing about His purposes.

## Jesus Christ

In our last section, we dealt mainly with refutations of naturalistic and idealistic philosophies, although theological schools of thought such as liberalism, God-is-dead theology, and critical theology as a whole were often referred to. In this section we will deal more specifically with individual theological views.

We have already noted that non-biblical theologies and philosophies agree in not accepting the Deity of Jesus. Yet, we have also seen that such Deity is demanded by a study of Jesus' teachings concerning His own Person, which were verified by God's raising Him from the dead. Thus, based on the resurrection, we affirm the Deity of Jesus (as we did in Chapter 3).

Nineteenth-century liberals were involved in a quest for the historical Jesus, minus the supernatural elements.[7] Liberalism often agreed with Kantianism that the most important element in Christology was stressing Jesus as a moral example for men. Thus, historical and ethical concerns dominated liberal studies of Jesus' life. In this century, some scholars are also interested in a new quest for the historical Jesus.[8] Less history is found in Christ's life and this history is not viewed as being decisive for faith, yet the revived interest in history is discernible.

Other contemporary theological schools of thought oppose such interest in history of any sort. Following Lessing and Kierkegaard, they hold that whether evidences are available or not, one must accept Christianity by a leap of faith and not because of any apologetics. Such is the view of neo-orthodoxy, represented by scholars such as Karl

---

[7]We have already refuted the naturalistic theories against the resurrection by such liberal scholars.

[8]Bornkamm and James Robinson, whose works we have dealt with above, are examples of such "new quest" scholars.

Barth, and of more existential theologies like those of Rudolf Bultmann and Paul Tillich. These views agree that Christ is affirmed by faith. Many contemporary theologians also deny the validity of the resurrection.

What does the historicity of the resurrection coupled with Jesus' claims concerning His Person and message dictate about such approaches? Using this event, an obvious conclusion is that the supernatural cannot be separated from Jesus' life. He was raised from the dead. This refutes most critical theologies as a whole.

Additionally, we have seen that we can indeed know about the historical Jesus. Likewise, it is valid to cite Jesus as a moral example for our lives. Yet the resurrection disproves liberalism both by its occurrence and by its substantiation of Jesus' Deity, which is denied by liberals. Thus Jesus is not only a historical Person and a moral example, but Deity as well.

Our conclusions likewise disprove neo-orthodoxy, existentialism, and post-existential views such as the new quest for the historical Jesus. We have perceived not only that the historical Jesus can be known, but also that the historical resurrection serves as a valid and much needed foundation for Christianity. Therefore, we must not only affirm Christ by faith, but show that this decision rests on a strong evidential basis.[9]

Contemporary existential scholars also hold that we are quite limited in our knowledge of God. But we would assert that Christ has revealed His Father so that we can, indeed, know more about Him.

Summarizing briefly, we have seen that the combination of Jesus' resurrection with His claims concerning His Deity and message provide us with a valid Christology. This

---

[9]See Habermas, *The Resurrection of Jesus: A Rational Inquiry*, pp. 198-224 for other problems with these critical approaches.

event and the subsequent demonstration of Jesus' Deity by God are two facts which disprove the views of most critical schools of thought. We thus saw that Jesus is not only a historical and moral figure, although these are true, but that He is also Deity. Likewise, views which downplay or deny the validity of the historical Jesus or other evidences are also incorrect. The resurrection plus Jesus' testimony do give us a firm historical foundation for our faith and also reveals limited, although by no means exhaustive, knowledge about God.

## Man and Salvation

Liberalism followed idealistic philosophy in postulating the essential goodness of man. Mankind was getting better and thus did not have to contemplate such a concept as a sinful nature.

Neo-orthodoxy and existentialism reacted strongly against this de-emphasis of sin by the liberals. These schools of thought sought to restore the importance of sin for Christian theology, though they still did not accept a historical Fall of man.

Again, the historicity of the resurrection dictates that Jesus' teachings are true. Jesus preached that man was sinful and thus He came to die an atoning death to pay for that sin. Only by repentance from sin and by a faith commitment in Christ's Person, substitutionary death, and resurrection can this sin be forgiven and eternal life gained. This concept of salvation and entrance into the Kingdom of God was examined in Chapter 5 and found to be valid.

Therefore, we may assert that man is sinful due to a historical fall of man. There is a corresponding gulf between God and man. Because of this sin, it is evident that man is not intrinsically good but is in need of real salvation, based on Christ's finished work on the cross and His resurrection. And as Jesus preached, judgment and punishment await those who decide against God. On the other hand, an eternal life of blessing awaits those who respond in repentance and faith in Christ and His message.

Concerning liberalism, the concept of the goodness of man is thus disproven. Man is sinful and in need of salvation. Otherwise there is no valid explanation of Christ's coming and of His death, especially in light of Jesus' own message on this subject.

While neo-orthodoxy and existentialism confirm the reality of sin, it was mentioned that such confirmation is usually not based on man's real guilt due to a historical fall of man. Usually Genesis 3 is taken as a myth. Thus, Christ's message dictates a much stronger, historical view of the fall and subsequent sin nature than that which is often held by such contemporary scholars.

We should also note here our earlier discussion concerning the need for eternal punishment (see Chapter 5). It was especially common in liberalism, but also in twentieth-century theological trends, to believe either that all religions are equally valid ways to God, or that Christianity is the highest form of religion, while others are still accepted by God. Such tendencies to adopt universalism, whereby all persons are said to be saved, or syncretism, whereby the best features of the world religions are combined and considered to be truth, are not compatible with Jesus' exclusive message of salvation only in Himself, which rests on a personal decision. He believed and taught that He was the *only* means of entrance to God's kingdom.

Therefore, we conclude that Jesus' concept of salvation is the correct one, as confirmed by His being raised by God. Modern men find such teachings hard to grasp, but it is clearly found to be the correct solution in light of this verification of Jesus' message. Liberalism's concept of the goodness of man is therefore incorrect, as are views which do not properly conceive of the historical reality of sin and subsequent fall of man. Repentance and a faith-commitment to God through the Person and substitutionary death and resurrection of Jesus Christ is the only solution, as indicated by the message of Jesus.

We have briefly viewed a few key areas of theology and have shown how both theistic arguments and the combination of Jesus' resurrection and His claims about His Deity and message provide a firm foundation for Christian doctrine and how these two arguments refute world views which are contrary to conservative Christianity. Rather than turn to other doctrines at this time, we will examine the case for the total inspiration of Scripture in the next appendix in order to ascertain a wider basis for all of Christian theology.

## A Caution

Before turning to the question of the inspiration of the Scriptures, a caution should be made at this point. Our intention in this appendix is *not* to formulate a type of natural theology by arguing from the resurrection to Christian theology and then build an intricate theology apart from Scriptural revelation. That this is not our intent is shown in at least three ways.

First, the New Testament also utilizes similar argumentation (see the Introduction for several instances) and, therefore, our presentation here is not properly viewed as an extra-biblical, natural demonstration. In other words, these arguments are also found in the New Testament and are thus neither non-Christian nor extra-Christian. We have already shown how such arguments may be used to validate Christian theism even for the skeptic. Such provide a very probable basis for the Christian world view.

Second, we did not attempt to offer a theology in this appendix, but rather a refutation of world views. In other words, our primary purpose here was to show how non-Christian world views are refuted and not to formulate a systematic theology. To construe our efforts in the latter sense is to miss the key point in this appendix.

Third, we will be turning to the question of the inspiration of Scripture in the next appendix. There it will be our desire to ascertain if the resurrection provides a valid foundation for accepting the Scriptures as a totally trustworthy source. If we find that the resurrection does provide such a foundation, then we will attempt to show how the Scriptures, in turn, provide a wider basis for all of Christian theology and living. As such, they will also provide a further refutation of world views such as those raised above.

Since we specifically mentioned this motive in the last section above, we repeat that our attempt is not to encourage the development of a system of natural theology apart from the Scriptures.[10] Some of the dangers involved in such a system will be given in the next appendix. Rather, we will seek to use Jesus' resurrection as the apologetic foundation for the trustworthiness of all of Scripture. The Scriptures, in turn, will then be able to give us an expanded basis for all of Christian belief.

---

[10]It is true that in this work we have argued from the resurrection to the truthfulness of several specific doctrines. For the validity of such an approach and the fact that this is not a system of natural theology, see the section on natural theology in the next appendix.

# The Inspiration of
# the Scriptures

We have already validated the principle that God verified Jesus' entire message by raising Him from the dead (see Chapter 3). In this appendix, we will examine Jesus' teachings on the inspiration of the Scriptures. According to our principle, we assert that if Jesus taught the total trustworthiness of the Scriptures, then we can trust Jesus' view as truth.

This subject is a very important one today, especially in light of contemporary questions. Although many try to downplay or deny such inspiration, we will endeavor to accept Jesus' teachings in this area, since His view has been verified by God through His resurrection.

### Jesus' Teachings on the Old Testament

The gospels record many statements of Jesus' concerning the inspiration and trustworthiness of the Scriptures. They agree unanimously that He had total confidence in the entire Old Testament. An inductive examination of Jesus' teachings will reveal His views on this subject.

One of Jesus' strongest statements concerning the trustworthiness of the Old Testament Scriptures occurred during His Sermon on the Mount. After having affirmed that He would fulfill the law and the prophets rather than abolish them, Jesus stated that not even so much as the smallest portion of a letter[1] of the law would be abrogated. Heaven and earth would pass away before such a minute fraction of the law would be made untrustworthy (Matt. 5:17–18).

In a similar and possibly even stronger statement, Jesus also taught that not even these smallest portions of letters would ever fail (Luke 16:17). Again, Scripture as a whole cannot be annulled or falsified (John 10:35).

Besides such specific comments on the total trustworthiness of Scripture, it is also instructive to notice some of Jesus' designations for the Old Testament. In Mark 7:8–13 Jesus referred to it as the "commandment of God" in a debate with the Pharisees and scribes (vv. 8, 9). Later, He also called the Old Testament the "Word of God" (v. 13). Such names plainly show that Jesus believed that the Old Testament was God's words and commandments to man.

Jesus also utilized the title "Scripture" (Mark 12:10; Matt. 22:29; John 5:39; 10:35) and asserted that it must be fulfilled (Matt. 26:54; Luke 4:21; John 7:38). This indicates further that it was inspired by God, since writings of man could not claim such authority.

Many times Jesus referred to Scripture in a discussion or confrontation with those who opposed His ministry. As

---

[1]In both Matt. 5:18 and Luke 16:17, the reference to a "jot" or "tittle" is usually taken to be the smallest portion of a Hebrew letter, a mark that distinguishes one letter from another (see Vine, *An Expository Dictionary of New Testament Words,* volume II, p. 277, volume IV, p. 140).

such, it became a sort of "proof text" for Him. Probably the best known example of this concerns His temptation in the wilderness where He quoted portions in opposition to Satan (Matt. 4:4, 7, 10). Other times Jesus would respond by asking "Have you not read . . ."[2], thereby citing Scripture as a definitive authority. Often the statement "It stands written . . ."[3] served as a refutation of an opposing view. In Matt. 22:29 we are additionally told that a knowledge of Scripture can keep us from error.

From the foregoing we can see that Jesus used the Old Testament as a proof text to show that His views were correct. It disproved the opinions of those who held contrary positions. It clearly was used as an authority and Jesus did not doubt this authority.

Jesus referred to the entire Old Testament both as the law and the prophets (Matt. 5:17) and as the law, prophets, and Psalms (Luke 24:44).[4] By either designation, Jesus plainly accepted the inspiration of each section as the Word of God. Moses, who is said to be the author of the Law (cf. Luke 16:31; 24:44), spoke God's words (Matt. 22:31, 32; Mark 12:26; cf. Exod. 3:16). David, in Psalm 110, spoke by the inspiration of the Holy Spirit (Mark 12:36). The prophets also spoke God's words, as indicated by the fact that prophecies of Christ had to be fulfilled (Luke 24:27, 44).

The gospels also assert that Jesus utilized the Old Testament as the source for solving theological disputes. It is related that on at least two occasions Jesus built His case chiefly on one word in the text. In Mark 12:35-37 He based His point on the second usage of the word "Lord" in

---

[2]Examples of this or similar statements see Mark 2:25; 12:10, 36; Matt. 19:4; 21:16.
[3]See Mark 9:12, 13; 11:17; 14:21, 27; Luke 7:27; etc.
[4]For a comparison and study of these two phrases, see Harris, *Inspiration and Canonicity of the Bible*, pp. 272-283.

order to show that the Messiah was more than the son of David. In Matthew 22:31, 32 Jesus built His argument on the word *am* in order to teach the truth of the resurrection of the body. Such confidence in the very words of Scripture further depicts Jesus' high view of inspiration.

Not only did Jesus affirm the inspiration of the entire Old Testament and the sections, but as we observed briefly above, He even taught the total inspiration of the words, letters and portions of letters (Matt. 5:18; Luke 16:17). Therefore, Jesus accepted the inerrancy of the Scriptures, since they could not be abrogated (John 10:35) and not even a section of a letter could fail (Luke 16:17). Such would not be affirmed by Jesus unless the Scriptures were inerrant.

At first one might wonder why Jesus would rely on such a written source when He realized that He was the very Son of God Himself. In other words, why would Jesus not simply speak by His own authority and not have to depend on a book written by men?

The answer to this query is twofold. We have seen throughout this work that Jesus did speak from His own authority many times. This is probably most obvious in Matt. 5:21ff., where Jesus countered both human corruption of the Scriptures and honored tradition with such words as "You have heard it said in old times ... but I say unto you. ..."[5] Thus He does rely on His own authority as a valid source.

In addition, Jesus relied on the Old Testament not because it was a time-honored, ancient source written merely by men. Rather, He realized that it was the very command and Word of God (Mark 7:8-13). Men certainly penned the words, but they were inspired by God (see Mark

---

[5]For a good explanation of how Jesus is opposing the teachings of men here and not Old Testament sayings, see the excellent discussion by Harris, Ibid., pp. 48-57.

12:36). Therefore, when He cited the Scriptures, He was making reference to the message of God. As such, He was using a final Source.

We therefore conclude that Jesus did accept the inspiration of the entire Old Testament.[6] It was an authority and proof text simply because it was the very Word of God (Mark 7:8-13). Such a conclusion is warranted by Jesus' specific statements that Scripture could not fail, pass away, or be falsified (Matt. 5:18; Luke 16:17; John 10:35). This conclusion can also be verified by a study both of Jesus' designations for Scripture and His use of it in disproving incorrect views.

In the whole and in the individual sections and portions, the Old Testament was God's Words and commandments to men. It is indeed noteworthy that Jesus extended this inspiration to the very parts of the letters of the text (Matt. 5:18; Luke 16:17), thereby teaching the Scriptures' inerrancy.[7]

### Jesus' Teaching on the New Testament

It is obvious to those who have studied Jesus' view of the trustworthiness of Scripture that the inspiration of the New Testament must be dealt with differently than that of the Old Testament. This difference lies in the fact that the former was not written until after Jesus' death. In spite of what might seem at first like a very difficult situation, we will argue for the validity of the as yet unwritten New Testament. Such an argument rests on four points.

---

[6]For an exceptional discussion of Jesus' view of the inspiration of Scripture, see Robert Lightner's book *The Saviour and the Scriptures* (Grand Rapids: Baker Book House, reprint 1978).

[7]In section C of this appendix we will turn to the question of validating the inspiration of Scripture for critics who question some of the references above as being the exact words of Jesus.

First, as with our study of the Old Testament, so we begin here with the facticity of Jesus' resurrection, as pointed out in Chapter 2. Based upon this foundation, we may accept the validity of Christ's teachings, since God verified and approved them by raising Christ from the dead. From this principle we turn now to His teaching concerning the future writing of the New Testament.

Second, Jesus made a twofold promise to His disciples concerning their future inspiration. He told them both that they would be His chosen spokesmen and that they would be inspired by the Holy Spirit. We will look briefly at each of these promises.

Jesus chose His disciples to learn of His teachings so that they, in turn, might go out and properly teach these same principles to others. As such, the disciples were Christ's witnesses (Luke 24:28; Acts 1:8; John 15:27). Accordingly, those who received the word of the disciples would actually be receiving Christ (Matt. 10:40; John 13:18, 20).

Jesus also promised the guidance of the Holy Spirit to His disciples. The Holy Spirit would teach them things that Jesus could not say at that time (John 16:12, 13), help them to remember Jesus' words (John 14:26) and reveal future things to them (John 16:13). In all these items, the Holy Spirit would lead the disciples unto all truth (John 16:13).

Thus, the disciples were Jesus' chosen spokesmen by virtue of their being taught by Jesus Himself, who said that they would be His witnesses. Jesus additionally promised that the Holy Spirit would help facilitate the disciples' roles as His witnesses, especially by bringing Jesus' words back to their remembrance. Probably most important, by leading the disciples to *all* truth in such matters (John 16:13), Jesus was asserting their inerrancy in the area of inspiration. This twofold promise by Jesus therefore insured the fact that the disciples would be His spokesmen. In this task they were inspired by the Holy Spirit.

Third, the New Testament writers personally claimed Jesus' twofold promise of inspiration for themselves. The apostles spoke the words of Christ (I Cor. 2:13; II Peter 3:2; Heb. 2:3, 4), which became the foundation of the Christian church (Eph. 2:20). Such witnessing of Christ's teachings was done in the power of the Holy Spirit and not in man's power (Eph. 3:3–5; I Peter 1:12; I Thess. 1:5). Other examples of these claimed promises are also evident, especially in the works of Paul.[8]

Fourth, the New Testament writers personally claimed Jesus' promise of inspiration for each other. For instance, Paul gives two quotes in I Tim. 5:18, referring to them both as Scripture. The first quote is plainly taken from Deut. 25:4. While the second quote has some conceptual similarities with the Old Testament, it is quoted nowhere. Actually, this reference is from Luke 10:7 (cf. Matt. 10:10). In comparing a quote from the Law to one in the gospels and by calling them both Scripture, Paul is certainly laying a foundation for the inspiration and canonicity of the New Testament (and the gospels and Acts in particular), especially when we remember the most sacred character of the Law for a Jew.

Another example is found in II Peter 3:15–16, where Paul's epistles are given the status of Scripture on a par with the other Scriptures. We might additionally point out that Jude 17–18 quotes II Peter 3:3 as the work of an apostle.

From I Tim 5:18 and II Peter 3:15–16 we get a glimpse not only of the recognition of inspiration for New Testament authors, but we also see the beginnings of the formu-

---

[8]See also I Cor. 14:37; Gal. 1:8–12; I Thess. 2:13.

lation of a canon of such inspired works. It is quite interesting to note that these two references specifically point to the inspiration and canonicity of the gospels, Acts, and Paul's epistles. These two groups of books were the earliest to be recognized as part of the New Testament canon, the first steps of which appear in the first century A.D. (mostly in these verses) and in the early second century.[9]

Therefore, we conclude that the inspiration and subsequent canonicity of the New Testament rests on the validated teachings of Jesus, who promised the disciples both that they were His chosen witnesses and that they would be led to all truth and inspired by the Holy Spirit. The New Testament authors claimed this twofold promise both personally for their own writings and on behalf of other qualified authors.[10] In this way we see the progression in the inspiration and canonicity of the New Testament.

## Accommodation or Limitation?

Sometimes it is charged that Jesus did not really accept this view of inspiration personally, but that He merely accommodated Himself to the beliefs of His contemporaries concerning this subject. In other words, although not holding to this belief in inspiration Himself, He spoke as if He did so that he did not upset the concepts or

---

[9]We cannot discuss the canonicity of the New Testament in the scope of this book. But the interested reader is referred to F. F. Bruce, *The New Testament Documents: Are They Reliable?* (Grand Rapids: William B. Eerdmans Publishing Company, 1960), especially pp. 21-28 and Harris, *Inspiration and Canonicity of the Bible*, pp. 197-294 for some of the information spoken of here.

[10]In light of the verified inspiration of the New Testament, it is also interesting to note its acceptance of the inspiration of the Old Testament. For examples, see II Tim. 3:16; II Peter 1:21; Gal. 3:15-16; Rom. 9:17; Acts 1:16; 28:25; Heb. 10:15-17.

undermine the views of the people of His day. It is also charged that Jesus Himself was limited in knowledge and thus accepted this view of inspiration without realizing that it was incorrect. Here it is said to be due to His lack of knowledge on this issue. Several refutations of each of these suggestions reveal that they are quite improbable.

Concerning the thesis that Jesus accommodated Himself to His hearers, it should be mentioned first that it was shown especially in Chapters 2 and 3 that God approved of Jesus' Person and teachings. For God to approve of what would, at best, be misleading teachings certainly is problematical, especially in that God does not lie.[11] Because of God's approval of Jesus' teachings, we have a strong refutation of the accommodation theory.

Another strong objection concerns the fact that, in other matters, Jesus did not accommodate His message to His hearers. On many occasions He *did* undermine the views of His audiences. This is probably most obvious, again, in His Sermon on the Mount in Matt. 5:21–48 where He constantly challenged the beliefs of His contemporaries. Other examples are also common in Jesus' teachings.[12] These distinctly show how Jesus did not accommodate His message to His hearers, but challenged incorrect beliefs which they held.

Jesus often spoke against false prophets,[13] once again showing that to follow their teachings was quite dangerous and misleading. This is obviously incompatible with the notion that He accommodated Himself to His hearers by confirming incorrect doctrine.

Two other points might be mentioned here as well.

---

[11]See Heb. 6:18 and our discussions above on God's Person and character (Chapters 2 and 3).
[12]For examples, see Mark 7:6–16; Matt. 12:9–14; 15:1–14; 22:23–33; 23:1–37; Luke 6:24–26.
[13]See Mark 13:21–23; Matt 7:15; 24:11 for examples.

Many times Jesus emphasized the usage of Scripture and referred to it as God's message.[14] Additionally, on several occasions Old Testament illustrations provided an argument for His viewpoint.[15] Both of these last points are also much more compatible with Jesus' total trust in the Scriptures.

Concerning the view of limitation, a very strong refutation once again concerns Jesus' claims that His message was directly from God,[16] as was shown in Chapters 2 and 3. As such, His testimony was not in error due to any limitation. Rather, His word was authoritative and constituted the truth, as indicated by God raising Jesus from the dead. Again, this event was God's stamp of approval on these teachings, which were therefore correct.

Another decisive refutation of this thesis is that even *after* Jesus' resurrection when He would have completely overcome any such human limitations, Jesus still held to to the same view of the Scriptures which He taught earlier (see especially Luke 24:25-27, 44-48). Thus, even when limitation is not a viable thesis, Jesus still held to the total inspiration and authority of the Word of God.

Finally, even before His death and resurrection, Jesus exercised supernatural knowledge.[17] This also militates against His being limited in knowledge.

Therefore, we conclude that both accommodation and limitation theories with regard to Jesus' teachings on inspiration are incorrect for several reasons.[18] Concerning the accommodation thesis, it was found that God's approval of Jesus' teachings through the resurrection would strongly

---

[14]See Mark 7:8-13; Matt. 4:4-11; Luke 4:4-13; cf. footnotes 2 and 3 above.

[15]For instance, see Matt. 12:39-40; Matt. 19:3-9; Luke 17:26-30.

[16]Again, see Matt. 11:27; 24:35; Luke 10:22; John 8:26-29, 42; 12:19-50; 13:3.

[17]For examples, see Mark 8:31; 9:31; 13:1-2; Luke 5:4-8; John 1:47-51; 2:24-25; 4:17-19; 6:64; 11:11-15; 18:4.

[18]For more indepth refutations, see John Wenham, *Christ and the Bible* (Downers Grove: Intervarsity Press, 1973); for a briefer treatment see John Wenham's essay "Christ's View of Scripture" in *Inerrancy,* edited by Norman Geisler. See also Geisler, *Christian Apologetics,* pp. 357-361.

militate against any such misleading practices. Also, Jesus did not accommodate His teachings but challenged and rebuked His listeners on many occasions. Additionally, Jesus' exhortations against false prophets are also incompatible with His own teaching if He accommodated the people. Finally, Jesus' use of the Old Testament indicates a strong approval of it, not just an attempt to appease people.

Concerning any limitation theses, God's raising Jesus again vindicates Jesus' testimony concerning Scripture and reveals that His view was not incorrect because of limited knowledge. This is also evident in that the *risen* Jesus displays the same confidence in Scriptures in spite of *not* being limited. Lastly, Jesus' supernatural knowledge on other matters shows that He was not limited.

## Critical Theology and Inspiration

It may be questioned by certain scholars whether some of the references above are the exact words of Jesus. In response, it should be mentioned that even by critical methods one may ascertain the fact that Jesus accepted the total trustworthiness of Scripture. It is for this reason that many critical theologians also recognize that Jesus believed that the Scriptures were inspired.

For example, Bultmann asserts that Jesus did not contest the authority of Scripture, but accepted it. For Jesus, God's will had been declared in the Old Testament and thus it was a valid source for one's life and for doctrine. As such, it was used as Jesus' source for answering questions and pointing out errors in the positions of those who opposed Him.[19]

---

[19]Bultmann, *Theology of the New Testament*, volume I, see pp. 15–17 for these assertions and for some of the references of Jesus' which Bultmann uses to support his view.

Brunner also notes that the validity of Scripture rests on the acceptance of its authority by Jesus and by its witness to Him. Although Brunner rejects verbal inspiration, he additionally relates that this was the view of some of pre-Christian Judaism, of Paul and of the other apostles. The earliest church always accepted the complete authority of the Old Testament and also added the New Testament from the time of the second century onwards.[20]

From this and other such instances[21] we can ascertain that critical scholars are also agreed that Jesus taught the total trustworthiness of the Scriptures. Although this doctrine is often rejected by such theologians in spite of Jesus' view, we now' have a solid ground on which to accept it. Since we have determined that Jesus' teachings included the inspiration of the Scriptures, according to both evangelical and other contemporary scholars, we may thus affirm this inspiration as being verified by God in His raising Jesus from the dead.

## The Importance of Inspiration

We saw that Jesus accepted the authority of the Old Testament, thus approving of its total trustworthiness. Since He affirmed the inspiration of even the smallest portions of the letters (Matt. 5:18; cf. Luke 16:17) and taught that Scripture cannot be falsified (Luke 16:17; cf. John 10:35), His view demands the teaching of the inerrancy of the Scriptures.[22]

---

[20]Brunner, *Dogmatics,* volume I, pp. 44–46, 106–108.
[21]Cf. also Bruce Metzger's article "Inspiration" in F. C. Grant and H. H. Rowley, *Dictionary of the Bible,* pp. 419–420; G. C. Berkouwer, *Studies in Dogmatics: Holy Scripture,* translated and edited by Jack Rogers (Grand Rapids: William B. Eerdman's Publishing Company, 1975), see pp. 148–149 for the authority of Scripture according to Christ.
[22]Lightner, *The Saviour and the Scriptures,* pp. 73–75.

Jesus also provided for the inspiration of the New Testament by His twofold promise to the disciples that they would both be His chosen witnesses and that they would be inspired by the Holy Spirit. In this manner the disciples would be led into all truth and thus kept from error (John 16:13). That the New Testament authors accepted Jesus' claims both for themselves and for the other writers further shows the effectiveness of Jesus' twofold promise.

Thus we conclude that we have a firm foundation for the inspiration of the Scriptures, both the Old and New Testaments. This foundation is Jesus' resurrection and the corresponding confirmation which it gives the testimony of Jesus, especially concerning inspiration. Therefore, in spite of contemporary doubts on this doctrine, we assert that since the basis is verified, so the doctrine remains valid. As asserted by former Princeton scholar Benjamin B. Warfield, as long as the evidence for inspiration is unrefuted, so-called errors in Scripture can only be counted as difficulties to which we must adjust our views.[23] In other words, as long as our basis remains validated (in this case it is our evidence from Jesus' resurrection and His testimony concerning inspiration), so-called discrepancies cannot be counted as errors, but must be dealt with otherwise.

It is our desire to turn briefly to the importance of this doctrine, as its truthfulness certainly has ramifications for all of Christianity. Indeed, just as the resurrection combined with Jesus' testimony provides the foundation for inspiration, so the inspiration of Scripture in turn provides a wider basis for Christian theology and life as a whole.

Earlier we perceived that Jesus utilized the Scriptures as a proof text in order both to substantiate His own views

---

[23]See Benjamin B. Warfield, *The Inspiration and Authority of the Bible* (Philadelphia: Presbyterian and Reformed Publishing Company, 1948), p. 174.

and to refute the positions of others which were contrary to the truth. He relied on Scripture in this way because it was the very Word of God, thereby giving Divine authority to its statements.

This benefit is also extended to us. We can build theology on the Scriptures, knowing that its doctrines and precepts are those of God Himself. Likewise, we can also utilize it as a guide with which we may evaluate the positions and world views of others. Based on the example of Jesus, Scripture can be both our theological absolute and our ruler for living a Christian life. In both respects, it is affirmed to be inerrant by Jesus.

This is our conclusion in this appendix, although we will also investigate some of the dangers of natural theology. This last study will also emphasize the importance of having a firm Scriptural basis for our theology.

## The Dangers of Misusing Natural Theology

Natural theology may generally be defined as the attempt to base a system of theology upon God's natural revelation to man. Historically, such approaches were often exercised in the form of deductions based on God's creation, the world, or "innate principles" of the human mind. Such approaches were often formulated in contrast to systems based on revealed theology. This practice was especially popular during the Enlightenment and was often manifest in rationalism and deism.

Even though certain older forms of natural theology have more or less died out, natural theologies are still popular today in some schools of thought. Such contemporary approaches are usually also contrasted with theologies based on special revelation.

It should be mentioned that certain arguments of

natural theology can have a valid place in Christian theology[24] and are even referred to in Scripture (see Ps. 19:1; Rom. 1:19-20). However, even contemporary attempts at utilizing natural theology as a substitute for special revelation have led to various problems.

For instance, the tendency of some scholars to stress and even accept only such data as can be gleaned from natural theology includes the implicit danger of causing one to believe that unless one can substantiate a doctrine by such methods, then perhaps that belief should be rejected or at least seriously questioned. At any rate, natural theologians usually agree in not accepting special revelation as a viable avenue for building theology.

The problem with such approaches is clear in terms of this study. Since God substantiated Jesus' message by raising Him from the dead, Jesus' teaching, in turn, verified the inspiration and inerrancy of the Old and New Testaments. Therefore, based on God's verification, such special revelation in Scripture can provide us with a firm ground on which to base our life and doctrine.

With such a comprehensive basis for accepting theology, it is obvious that natural theology has often failed to utilize such special revelation in its methodology. Therefore, in rejecting this revelation, much knowable truth is also rejected or ignored.

This is a major weakness in natural theologies. The Scriptures, which are validated by Jesus' resurrection and teachings, thereby substantiate the theology it teaches. To reject or ignore this theology is to leave out much, perhaps even a crucial amount, of Christianity. At the least, a large percentage of truth is being ignored.

An additional problem is that whenever a philosophy is

---

[24]An example in this work would be our presentation of the cosmological arguments in Chapter 2.

aligned too closely with Christianity, some truths are often compromised. We have just seen a broad example of this in certain rejections of Scripture. But it is also true that when the philosophy goes out of style and loses popularity, some think that the theology loses its significance too. Such an assessment is also invalid, as pointed out above.

These are some of the weaknesses of natural theologies which are not strongly linked to the special revelation of the Scriptures. To repeat, a large and perhaps even crucial amount of Christianity is thereby neglected.

It would be advantageous to comment once again on the validity of our arguments from the resurrection to Christian theology. First, as already stated above, since such argumentation is also often utilized in Scripture, we find that such approaches are neither non-Christian or extra-Christian. This is noteworthy because such an apologetic allows us to show that Christianity is valid even with those who do not grant Christian presuppositions and who utilize critical methods. The resurrection and corresponding theology are still verified even under such circumstances.

Second, by arguing from Jesus' resurrection to the inspiration of Scripture, as we did in this appendix, we are securing a foundation for theology as a whole—that of the inspired Scriptures. Thus we are not in danger of using apologetic arguments as a substitute for special revelation.

It could be misleading to present our apologetic system apart from the inspiration of Scripture because it might encourage others to do likewise. But we are plainly not doing this, since we combined the facticity of the resurrection with Jesus' testimony in order to show the inspiration of Scripture, thus giving us a much wider basis for Christian life and theology. In the Scripture we have both a "proof text" for our beliefs and a refutation of opposing positions.

# Eternal Life

In Chapters IV and V we studied Jesus' central teaching, that of the kingdom of God and its entrance requirements. In this appendix we will concentrate on one major facet of that message by examining the Christian view of eternal life. This is a most fascinating topic, especially in light of the current interest in death and life after death.

## The Resurrection of the Body Versus Immortality of the Soul

Before we turn to the nature of eternal life, we will compare and contrast several ancient views of the afterlife. These will come under two broad categories—the immortality of the soul and the resurrection of the body. This study will give us a background from which to present the Christian position.

## Immortality of the Soul

The view of the immortality of the soul was especially prevalent in Greek thought and in areas affected by Hellenism. A key influence here was that of Platonic philosophy. Briefly, the soul of man was said to have existed before the birth of the body, where it acquired knowledge in the eternal realm of Ideas. The body, on the other hand, was earthly and part of the world of the senses. Because man was made up of both body and soul, he was born with a vast knowledge gained from the eternal realm, although such information was difficult to recall because of the influence of the body and its earthly cravings. Nonetheless, the soul itself was not wicked and could never be destroyed by evil.

The body was the temporary vehicle for the soul, but actually hindered the soul and even imprisoned it by its material nature and desires. Thus, the proper practice was to control the body and avoid its lusts in order for the soul not to be hindered any more than necessary. However, pure knowledge was still impossible in this life because of the body.

At death the body died while the soul, after being reborn many times over thousands of years, was finally freed to take its flight to the eternal realm where it would make its abode. Here, personal immortality would be experienced in a life characterized by bliss and the obtaining of pure wisdom.[1]

Greek thought was much influenced by Plato, especially in this concept of the realm of Ideas and immortality of the soul. Gnosticism, for instance, adopted similar concepts, although more stress was placed on the actual evil charac-

---

[1]These ideas are taught in many of Plato's writings, such as *Phaedo, Meno,* the *Republic,* and *Phaedrus.*

ter of the body. Neo-Platonism was basically a later and more mystical development of related views.

In ancient philosophy, various versions of these theories were quite popular. This was perhaps even the view of the majority of thinkers in the Mediterranean area in ancient times.

## The Resurrection of the Body: The Old Testament View

Also popular among ancient peoples was the concept of cyclical history popularized by the Greeks and others. This view theorized that history did not actually progress in a forward direction but repeated itself, especially corresponding to the cycles of nature.

Contrary to this, the Jews conceived of history as a linear process. God had worked in past history, illustrated especially by their exit from Egypt and subsequent journeys. These acts of God were recalled often (See Pss. 78, 106 for examples). God was also acting at present and would act in the future, such as in establishing His Kingdom and eternal life (cf. Dan. 7).

Throughout their history, the Jews believed in life after death. In earlier works, this was expressed as existence in Sheol, or the place of the shadows. It was an existence where life was not really satisfied (Prov. 27:20) and from which there was no return (Job 7:9). The wicked would be in Sheol (Ps. 49:14) and there would be no real fellowship with God (Isa. 38:18). Neither would there be any activity, planning or wisdom there (Eccles. 9:10).

These negative aspects of Sheol are often stressed by commentators, usually without mention of some of the more positive aspects which are associated with it. For example, it is related that God does save men from Sheol (Ps. 16:8-11) and that God is present there (Ps. 139:8). It is even inferred that peace is found in Sheol (I Sam. 28:15).

It is quite possible that the Jews believed that there were separate places in Sheol for the righteous and the unrighteous. For instance, Psalm 49:13-15 contrasts the difference between the wicked and the righteous in Sheol. In fact, the pseudepigraphal Book of Enoch (22:9-13) does teach such a division of persons.

At any rate, the Jews became increasingly aware of the prospect of a blessed existence after death for the righteous. Through progressive revelation, God led His followers to the conviction that the body would be transformed and raised at the end of history.[2] The unrighteous would experience judgment at this time as well.

In the Old Testament, the examples of Enoch (Gen. 5:24) and Elijah (II Kings 2:11) being taken to heaven bodily do not actually teach a resurrection of the body, but certainly have some similarities. They certainly could have helped cause the Jews to realize that God had a place of blessing prepared for the righteous.

The two clearest places in the Old Testament which explicitly teach a bodily resurrection are Isa. 26:19 and Dan. 12:2-3. The former presents the time of the resurrection of the body as a joyous occasion (cf. Isa. 25:8), while the latter speaks both of those who are being raised to an eternal life of glory and those who are raised to everlasting disgrace. In these instances we have the clear teaching that the righteous will be raised bodily to live eternally in a state of blessedness.[3]

Before leaving the subject of the resurrection of the body in the Old Testament, we might also quickly note two other areas of interest. First, the apocryphal books differ in their presentation of eternal life. Ecclesiasticus lacks a

---

[2]Cf. Floyd F. Filson, "Resurrection" in Grant and Rowley, *Dictionary of the Bible,* p. 843.

[3]For a summary comparison of the Greek and Hebrew beliefs on the question of eternal life, see Filson, "Resurrection," Ibid, pp. 843-844.

clear presentation of any blessed future existence and appears to speak of an existence like that in Sheol (14:16; 22:11; 46:19, etc.). The Wisdom of Solomon seems to teach the immortality of the soul (2:23; 3:1-10), while II Maccabees clearly teaches the resurrection of the body with the physical organs intact (especially 14:46; cf. 7:9; 12:43-45). Second, the pseudepigraphal books also present no unanimous opinion. The predominant view appears to be the resurrection of the body, sometimes in changed form (Apocalypse of Baruch 50:2-51:10; I Enoch 51:1-2; 62:13-16), although the fifth Book of Enoch seems to teach the immortality of the soul (103:4).[4]

We will conclude our survey of the Old Testament view of eternal life by stating that the early Jews conceived of such life in terms of Sheol, seemingly with distinctions between the states of the wicked and the righteous. However, as God's revelation progressed, the resurrection of the body became the dominant view. By the time of Jesus, this was also the predominant view, although a diversity of opinions existed.[5]

## The Resurrection of the Body: Jesus' View

The Jews in the time of Jesus also were not unanimous in their views of the afterlife. The Sadducees denied the resurrection (Acts 23:8) and challenged Jesus with their view (Mark 12:18-27). It is quite difficult to determine the view of the Essenes, especially since Josephus and Hippolytus disagree as to whether they accepted the immortality of the soul or the resurrection of the body. The Pharisees taught the resurrection of the body, as does the Talmud. Based on this evidence, we may conclude that the

---

[4]See Ladd, *I Believe in the Resurrection of Jesus,* pp. 51-59 for some very pertinent conclusions here.
[5]Cf. Ibid., p. 58.

teaching of the resurrection of the body was the dominant concept in Judaism in the first century A. D., as indicated by the views of the Pharisees, the Talmud, and other first century writings such as the Apocalypse of Baruch and IV Ezra.[6]

Jesus likewise taught the resurrection of the body. In a discussion with the Sadducees over the question of this subject, Jesus affirmed that the resurrection of the body was taught in the Old Testament, as God is the God of the living and not of the dead. Jesus additionally taught that those who are raised do not marry in heaven, but are like the angels (Mark 12:18-27).

Jesus further pointed out that all of the dead would be raised, some to eternal life and some to eternal punishment (Matt. 25:31-46; cf. John 5:28-29). He did comment briefly on the nature of this resurrection life. It will be life in the kingdom of God, which had been prepared for the righteous since before the world began (Matt. 25:34; John 14:1-3). Such life will be eternal (Luke 20:36) and will include personal fellowship (Matt. 8:11; Mark 14:25) and rewards (Luke 14:14). Generally, Jesus refers to this eternal blessedness simply as "life" (ζωή), thereby making reference to its quality of happiness (Mark 9:43, 45; 10:23, 30; Matt. 7:13-14).[7] Thus Jesus does teach the resurrection of the body, describing some of the characteristics of the subsequent eternal bliss for the righteous.[8]

It should be mentioned here briefly before continuing that Jesus' resurrection validates this Judeo-Christian con-

---

[6] See Ibid., and Filson, "Resurrection" in Grant and Rowley, *Dictionary of the Bible,* p. 844.

[7] Vine, *An Expository Dictionary of New Testament Words,* volume II, p. 336. It is noteworthy that in the gospel of John this eternal life is both a present possession (John 3:36; 6:47; etc) and a future reality (John 5:24; 11:25, 26; etc.), Ladd presents a very interesting study of this concept in John, noting that it is a different emphasis, but the same truth as taught by the synoptic gospels (*The Pattern of New Testament Truth,* pp. 64-86).

[8] For Bultmann's attestation to these beliefs of Jesus, see *Theology of the New Testament,* volume I, pp. 5-6 and *History and Eschatology,* pp. 32-33.

cept of the resurrection of the body, as opposed to the Greek concept of the immortality of the soul. This is both because God validated Jesus' teaching on this subject by raising Him and because Jesus was raised in a new body and thus did not experience Greek immortality.

## The Resurrection of the Body: The New Testament View

The New Testament also clearly teaches the resurrection of the body. This position was held against both the view of the Sadducees (Acts 4:2) and the Greek view of the immortality of the soul (Acts 17:32). For early Christians, there would be a future resurrection of both the righteous and the unrighteous (Acts 10:42; 24:15; Rom. 2:6-10). Jesus Himself was to be the judge (Acts 10:42; II Cor. 5:10).

The most indepth treatment of the nature of the resurrection life is Paul's account in I Cor. 15. The key concept here is that of the spiritual body. Men are raised in actual bodies, but they are changed (15:44, 50-54). Paul describes this resurrection body as being imperishable, glorified, powerful and spiritual in contrast to earthly bodies, which are just the opposite (vv. 42-44).

Paul argues, by analogy, that grain differs much from that which is harvested. Animals also have various kinds of bodies. Even celestial bodies are different from one another. Likewise, our resurrection bodies are different from our earthly bodies and perhaps even different from the resurrection bodies of other saved persons, depending on our crowns and rewards (15:35-42).[9]

In order to do justice to this Pauline phrase "spiritual body," we must stress both aspects of the resurrection

---

[9]This latter intriguing possibility is derived not only from Paul's analogy of distinction between earthly and heavenly bodies (I Cor. 15:40 in particular), but especially from his stress on various types of heavenly bodies, even those of the same kind (vv. 41-42).

body. It is a real body, but it has taken a new form from its earthly counterpart. Thus, we must realize that we are speaking of an actual body, but one that is changed.

The New Testament as a whole agrees in teaching the reality of the resurrection of the body.[10] For instance, Jesus rose with a new body, rather than having experienced the Greek concept of the immortality of the soul. He had a similar body and the same personality and was recognized as such. But He had new powers and He was not bound by time and space. He had a real body, but it was a new and glorified one (cf. Matt. 28:1-6; Luke 24:31, 36; John 20:19-20).

The early church held that Jesus' resurrection was an example of that of believers' (Rom. 6:5; I Cor. 15:22; I Thess. 4:14). Those who accepted Jesus' teachings would be changed in order to be like Him (I John 3:2). Thus, believers will have their earthly bodies transformed into glorious bodies like that of the risen Jesus (Phil. 3:20-21). Eternal life follows this transformation (II Cor. 5:1-10).

It might be mentioned here that in the New Testament, the resurrection power is not only future, but is present in the new life of the believer (John 3:3; I Peter 1:3; Titus 3:5). Thus Paul can claim that the power of the resurrection is available now (Phil. 3:10). We might conclude, therefore, that the New Testament teaches both a new power for our present lives (II Cor. 5:18-19; John 6:47) and a transformed, resurrected body of glory for our eternal life in the future age to come (I Cor. 15; II Cor. 4:14; 5:1-10; John 6:39-40).

### The Nature of Eternal Life

We have ascertained several times in this work that Jesus' message was that those who responded to His Per-

---

[10]Filson, "Resurrection" in Grant and Rowley, *Dictionary of the Bible*, p. 846.

son and teachings by exercising repentance and faith in Him would be admitted to God's eternal kingdom. We will now look briefly at the New Testament teaching on the nature of the resurrection life.

Jesus taught that the kingdom of God had been prepared for the righteous since before the world began (Matt. 25:34; John 14:1-3). Paul asserted that no one could even imagine the wonderful things that God has in store for believers (I Cor. 2:9). The Book of Revelation relates the exquisite beauties of the eternal state (Rev. 21, 22; cf. II Peter 3:10-13).

What is the nature of this eternal life in the kingdom of God? What will believers do there? Needless to say, it is not an endless life of simply playing harps and floating on clouds!

The New Testament does relate several aspects of eternal life and the activity there, although no one asserts that such is an exhaustive list. We are told that believers will worship God (Rev. 4, 5), serve God (Rev. 22:3) and reign with Him forever (Rev. 22:5). The eternal realm will also be a place of rest (John 14:1-3; Rev. 14:13) and personal fellowship with each other (Matt. 8:11; I Cor. 13:12; John 14:3).

One important aspect of eternal life is that the believer will progress in knowledge. This is the probable meaning of I Cor. 13:12, where Paul explains that learning in this life is progressive and partial (γινώσκω ἐκ μερους), while in the future eternal state our knowledge is still progressive, but more full and advanced (ἐπιγνώσομαι). This contrast points out that we will continue to learn, but in a more complete sense.[11]

The redeemed will also be able to share in God's new creation (Rev. 21:1). Revelation 21-22 speaks of its har-

---

[11]See Vine, *An Expository Dictionary of New Testament Words,* volume II, pp. 298-299.

mony of color (see 21:18-21) and other aspects of its character. This world will provide much enjoyment for the people of God, as indicated, for instance, by its dwelling places (John 14:2-3; Rev. 21:10-21) and beautiful scenery (see Rev. 22:1-2 for an example).

Closely related and equally exciting, God's new creation is referred to as Paradise (παραδείσῳ—Rev. 2:7), of which the garden of Eden is a type (Gen. 2:8). The idea is that of a beautiful garden (cf. Num. 24:6) characterized by exquisite blessedness.[12] This new world will be created for believers to dwell in and enjoy (cf. II Peter 3:13).

Eternal life will also be devoid of the negative qualities of this life, such as death, pain and sorrow (Rev. 21:4; cf. Isa. 25:8). Rather, it is characterized by holiness (Rev. 21:15, 27) and living in Christ's glory (Col. 3:4). For believers, it is in this eternal heaven that our citizenship lies (Phil. 3:20).

Again, this is by no means an exhaustive treatment of this subject. However, it does give us a glimpse of the glorious life ahead for those who have followed Christ in faith. As Paul taught, we cannot even begin to comprehend all the blessings of eternal life. But we can be sure that God has prepared wonderful things for His own (I Cor. 2:9). Jesus' resurrection has insured such an eternal life of bliss for believers.


## Jesus' Resurrection and Eternal Life


As we just perceived, Jesus' resurrection is an example of the believer's resurrection (I Cor. 15:21-22; Rom. 6:9). Therefore, this historical event assures us that we will be raised too (II Cor. 4:14). If Jesus had not risen, then we

---

[12]Ibid., volume III, pp. 158-159.

would have no basis for accepting the resurrection of the body (I Cor. 15:12, 18-19).

As such, the doctrine of the resurrection of the body which we have presented here rests on the reality of Jesus' resurrection. For this reason, our apologetic for this event, of which we gave a concise summary in Chapter 1, is most crucial. For instance, to repeat our earlier conclusion, the historicity of this event guarantees that the Judeo-Christian concept of the resurrection of the body is correct, as opposed to the Greek concept of the immortality of the soul. Now we may state a different application of this event, in that evidence for God's raising Jesus from the dead actually becomes evidence for the raising of believers as well.

The resurrection of Jesus provides a strong, twofold evidence for eternal life after death. First, in raising Jesus from the dead, God validated Jesus' teaching on the resurrection of the body and the subsequent eternal life, which we examined briefly above. Again, this validation especially applies to Jesus' teaching concerning eternal life, since it was His central message (see Chapters 4 and 5). Thus, the teachings about our eternal state have been verified. Second, we now perceive that Jesus' resurrection actually becomes an example of our raising. Eternal life is shown to be a reality. Just as He arose, so will believers.

Jesus' being raised from the dead conclusively demonstrates that death is not the end, but simply a transition to a new, everlasting life. Based on these reasons, we may assert that verification of Jesus' resurrection is likewise verification of the believers' eternal life.

The New Testament also holds that the chief verification of the believer's resurrection is Jesus' example (I Cor. 15:45-57). This event also provides our basis for victory over the fear of death (Heb. 2:14-15). Having concluded that the resurrection of Jesus is the chief demonstration of the resurrection of the body,[13] we will now turn to the question of victory over the fear of death in order to ascertain how this event does indeed give us a valid answer.

## Fear of Death

There is little doubt that the fear of death is probably the most basic and widespread fear known to man. Several reasons account for this condition. We will attempt to deal briefly with the most common aspects of this fear before addressing ourselves to the question of victory over it.

First, death involves the realm of the unknown. People like to know what is happening and where they are going, while death is seen as the chief obstacle to that knowledge.

Here we must admit, as we did above, that there is much we do not know about life after death. We cannot even imagine all its blessings (I Cor. 2:9). Yet we can be sure that Jesus has experienced death and that He emerged victorious by rising from the dead. By virtue of His resurrection, the realm of death is no longer unknown. True, we lack much knowledge concerning it, but the resurrection guarantees that an eternal life of blessedness is ahead for believers. We can rest assured that enough has been shown to us that we do know that it will be a totally positive existence.

Probably second only to the fear of the unknown is the fear of terminating our earthly relationships. We are naturally reluctant to want to leave our loved ones and so we fear death.

---

[13]There are several other good evidences for life after death, such as those based on prophecy in the Scriptures and certain scientific and philosophical arguments. However, a discussion of even the relevant facts would take us beyond the scope of this appendix.

Here it is important to remember Jesus' teachings that the afterlife will include personal fellowship with one another (Matt. 8:11). In fact, Paul states that our relationships will be complete only after death (I Cor. 13:12). In other words, we literally have to go through death in order to experience the ultimate fellowship with one another, including our loved ones.

Third, many fear the pain often associated with death. It is true that many times this pain is probably feared even more than death itself.

Paul addresses himself to such a question in a very informative discussion (II Cor. 4:7-5:1-10). Here he speaks of the afflictions that beset the human life (II Cor. 4:7-12), comparing the present suffering to the eternal glory that awaits the believer. Paul concludes that this suffering is minor in comparison to eternal life (II Cor. 4:17-5:4. True, pain is not easy to bear, but we must keep our eyes off such temporary situations and on eternal reality. Suffering can be endured when we know the blessings that follow this life.

Some fear a fourth aspect following death, namely, the judgment. This is especially the case when one realizes that his life is not what God intended that it might be.

The advice of the Scriptures in light of this promise of judgment is to be sure we respond correctly to God's invitation to follow Him in salvation while we are yet in these bodies (II Cor. 5:10-11; John 3:16-21, 36). Now is the time to accept Christ's message by faith (II Cor. 6:2). After death it is too late to try to respond in repentance and belief in God through the Person and work of Jesus Christ. Those who have already committed their lives and who are "in the Son" have no need to fear eternal punishment (I John 5:9-13).

Fifth, many fear the decomposition of this body which follows death. We often conceive of this physical body as our real self and identify ourselves with it.

We will only hint at a solution to this fear in order to deal with it at length in the next section of this appendix. Suffice it to say here that our physical body is not our real self (I Cor. 15:50–53). It is questionable if we can ever gain assurance of eternal life unless we understand this point. We must realize that our real self is what survives death. Therefore, we lose nothing which is integral to our future existence.

These five examples of worries only touch on the question of conquering this overall fear of death. By discussing these typical problem areas we are not actually getting at the root of the fear itself. We will endeavor to do that now in order to give this brief study of problems more meaning.

## Assurance of Eternal Life

In order to present our case for gaining victory over the fear of death, one key principle and three supportive points will be adduced. It should be kept in mind throughout that the validity of the historical resurrection of Jesus guarantees these propositions as a whole, as shown earlier in this appendix.

In conquering the fear of death, this author believes that a key principle is involved. That is, we must learn to recondition our attitudes toward death. Instead of looking at death as an inherent evil and as a completely negative entity, we must realize that it is a natural process of change to a higher form of spiritual life. In this sense we must learn to educate ourselves to look at death from God's perspective.

Admittedly, this principle is "easier said than done." For this reason, we will now introduce three supportive points which build on each other, in order to show how such a principle may be implemented personally. It must be remembered here that since our education is essentially a learning process, and because we have taught ourselves to fear death all of our lives, we must therefore learn to view death differently. This is what we will strive for here.

First, we must learn to think of our real selves as being distinct from our physical bodies. In other words, our present bodies are not the real "us." These physical organs are temporary, whereas our mind and spirit are eternal. Thus, while we are surely united to our bodies, we must be so only in order to operate in this earthly realm. Our spirit is distinct from and works through our body and brain.

Such a position is also taught in Scriptures. Man is a spiritual creature, created in God's own image (Gen. 1:26–27). Since God does not have a human, physical body (cf. John 4:24), being made in His image must refer primarily to having an immaterial nature. It follows, then, that the most important portion of man, that which is created in God's image, is our immaterial portion.

Accordingly, we can speak of our "inner man" not only as being distinct from our physical body, but it also can be said that while our body is dying, our spirit is unaffected (II Cor. 4:16). Even now we have our eternal form, although we have not been resurrected as such.

It should be cautioned at this point that while it is being asserted here that our real selves are not our physical bodies, this does not abrogate the need for or the importance of our bodies. Our material portion certainly helps mold our personalities and is definitely needed for life in this world. It must also be remembered here that in our final state we will be "clothed" with a new resurrection body like that of Jesus. Therefore, it must be understood in the proper context that, especially when speaking of death, our physical body is not our real self.[14]

---

[14]Therefore, we are not teaching gnostic ideas here, since, for instance, we are not viewing the body as being intrinsically evil as taught in that philosophy.

Second, after we have learned to think of our real selves as being distinct from our physical bodies, we must realize that, because of this distinction, we will remain living whether our body is dead or alive. The life of our real self is unaffected by the death of the body. As a result, we should view death as a harmless change to an eternal existence.

This will, of course, take practice on our part. But this second point is likewise based on the evidence we have, especially concerning Jesus' resurrection. Thus we must bring our beliefs into accord with this evidence, which dictates that we continue to live apart from our bodies. This idea must be stressed. Whatever happens to our physical body, we remain alive. Again, Scripture also supports this point that death does not affect our real selves (II Cor. 5:1; John 11:25-26).[15]

These first two points lead us to a third and concluding point. Because we are distinct from our physical bodies and live in spite of the death of these bodies, we must learn that death is therefore a transition to eternal life. It is not a cessation of life, but just the beginning of one's eternal existence. Thus, to die simply means that we are out of our physical body but alive and living with the Lord (II Cor. 5:8; cf. John 5:24).

Since death is a transition to eternal life, we can even view death as a great adventure. As related by Joseph

---

Neither are we teaching Platonism. This is because we are grounding our view in both the Old Testament and the New Testament, not in Greek philosophy. It should be remembered that everyone who believes that the spirit is separate from the body does not have to be Platonic. Our view differs from that of Plato in several respects (see section A above), not the least of which is the contrast between the resurrection of the body and the immortality of the soul.

[15]The New Testament example of Stephen is quite instructive here (Acts 7:59-60). Although Stephen's body was dead (v. 60), his spirit went to be with Jesus (v. 59). Ecclesiastes 12:6, 7 teaches the same, that while our body will return to dust, our spirit goes to be with God.

Bayly, "It is the Great Adventure, beside which moon landings and space trips pale in significance."[16]

This is an exciting prospect for the believer! Death is, indeed, an adventure from the realm of earth to the realm of heaven. Even though we do not understand all that is involved, we know enough not to fear it anymore.[17]

To summarize briefly, we must first understand that our real selves are distinct from our physical bodies. Our physical bodies are temporal, while we are eternal. Second, as we saw from this distinction, we remain living whether our bodies are dead or alive. The life of our real selves is actually unaffected by the death of the body. Third, we must learn to think of the death of our bodies not as the end, but as the transition to eternal life. It is actually a fantastic adventure to be experienced by all believers.

To apply these three points is to fulfill our key principle, which is to recondition our attitudes toward death. When we come to understand that death is a transition from earthly life to eternal life, then we are looking at this phenomenon from God's perspective.

By repeated references to learning a new attitude towards death, we are speaking of actually practicing these truths. The death of a loved one is not the time to begin training oneself not to fear death. Just as we have educated ourselves over the years to fear death, so we must now educate ourselves to the real truth about death. It is not to be feared, since believers live eternally without their physical bodies. Again, death is a transition to that eternal life.

The Scriptures also teach that we can have real assurance of life after death. We are told that we can actually

---

[16]Joseph Bayly, *The View from a Hearse* (Elgin: David C. Cook Publishing Company, 1969), p. 20; cf. p. 46.
[17]For an excellent treatment of issues such as these raised here, see C. S. Lovett, *Death Made Easy* (Published by Personal Christianity, Baldwin Park, California).

know that we have eternal live if we have believed in Christ
(I John 5:9-13). Likewise, we may know that at death we
will experience this new life (II Cor. 5:1). Later we will
be reunited with our resurrected body (I Cor. 15:50-53;
I Thess. 4:14-16). It is the death and resurrection of Christ
that gives us this victory over the fear of death, which has
held many in bondage all of their lives (Heb. 2:14,15).

Since we continue to live even immediately after death
(II Cor. 5:8; Phil. 1:21, 23; John 11:25-26; Luke 23:43),
we have no need to fear it at all. We may even look forward
to death (II Cor. 5:2; Phil. 1:20-23).

Such a view of death, once it has become embedded in
our thought and belief, can have many consequences in
our earthly lives. This assurance of eternal life can help us
perceive the death of a loved one, as well as our own, in a
much different and better light. We can even understand
the blessedness of the situation and not view it as an evil.
Also, it is probable that all Christians would live more
effective lives and be more committed to God if we could
be relieved of our own fear of death (Heb. 2:14-15). Most
obvious would be our own victory over this fear, leading to
peace in our own lives.

Based especially on the resurrection of Jesus, believers
therefore have a valid basis for their belief in eternal life
and their own future resurrection of their body (II Cor.
4:14). Thus our corresponding assurance of this eternal
life is also built on a solid foundation. This assurance can
be a reality in each of our lives as well.

# The Holy Spirit and Apologetics

In this appendix we will attempt to outline the crucial part that the Holy Spirit plays in apologetics. In so doing we will be further expanding portions of the Introduction to this book.

## Evidences and the Gospel

In the Introduction we briefly showed that in the New Testament various approaches were taken to the presentation of the gospel. Sometimes a straightforward proclamation of the gospel was given. Other times, reasoning and the giving of evidences paved the way for such a presentation.[1] We will expand our earlier treatment here by study-

---

[1] It is not the intention here to discuss the commonly debated presuppositional-evidential question in apologetics. Rather, the terms "evidential" or "evidences" as used in this book generally have reference to the reasonable presentation of the claims of Christianity without specifically applying to either methodological approach.

ing specific examples from Paul's ministry as presented in the Book of Acts. Our emphasis will primarily be on the instances where Paul employed evidences and logical persuasion with his listeners. This is both because such is the nature of this work and because some scholars oppose the use of apologetic reasoning in presenting the claims of Christianity.

Sometimes a direct presentation of the gospel led to the conversion of the listener. When Paul and his companions went out to a river bank and witnessed to Lydia, who worshiped God herself, the Lord led her to respond and accept the gospel (Acts 16:13-15).

Later, after being thrown into prison, Paul and Silas began praying and singing while the others present were listening. After an earthquake, the jailer asked what he had to do to receive salvation. After the explanation that he must believe in the Lord Jesus Christ, he acted in faith, as did his family (Acts 16:23-34).

In these two instances the person's heart had already been prepared by the Holy Spirit. Lydia was a worshiper of God and the Philippian jailer had apparently heard Paul's message through prayer and song. Both were ready for the gospel and readily accepted it.

However, in several other instances it was necessary to present evidences and careful persuasion for a person's heart to respond to the gospel. Paul went to Thessalonica and reasoned with the Jews from the Old Testament Scriptures that Jesus was prophesied to be the Messiah, concentrating on the death and resurrection of Jesus. Some were persuaded by this logical presentation to believe in Christ and they followed Paul (Acts 17:1-4). It is interesting to note here that on such occasions when Paul spoke to the Jews concerning Old Testament messianic prophecy, he utilized the presuppositions of his audience. Since they also accepted the Scripture, he used it as his starting point for presenting the gospel.

We have already looked at Paul's lecture at Areopagus. In the beginning he used his reasoning methods with the Jews and God-fearing Greeks in the synagogue and marketplace (Acts 17:17). Later, he confronted the skeptical Greeks with the message of the gospel. After speaking of God and His natural revelation, Paul spoke of the need for repentance in light of the coming judgment by Jesus. He concluded that these doctrines were all demonstrated by God's raising Jesus from the dead (17:22–34). It is quite noteworthy here that, rather than reason from Old Testament evidences such as prophecy as he did earlier, Paul established another area of agreement with these skeptics. This helped him to gain more acceptance for his statements concerning God, since he quoted Greek poets who agreed with certain of his facts, thus bolstering his position. As happened earlier, some were also persuaded to believe at Areopagus (v. 34).

In Corinth, Paul went to the synogogue, as at Thessalonica, in order to reason with the Jews and God-fearing Greeks (Acts 18:1–6). He argued that Jesus was the Messiah (18:4, 5), presumably using Old Testament prophecy once again.

At Ephesus he likewise employed apologetic persuasion. On an earlier trip he continued his custom of reasoning with the Jews (Acts 18:19). Later, he spent three months in the local synagogue reasoning and persuading men concerning the kingdom of God. When some hardened their hearts to his words, Paul withdrew to the school of Tyrannus, where he reasoned with and taught his hearers for two years. The result was that the gospel was heard throughout Asia (Acts 19:8–10).

Lastly, we will mention Paul's encounter with King Agrippa (Acts 26). This was primarily a one-on-one discussion, although others were present. In this situation Paul also appealed both to the Old Testament prophets and to Jesus' resurrection in order to validate his case (vv. 22–27).

It should be mentioned here that Paul's usage of various reasoning approaches is especially obvious from the words which were chosen to express his methods. In these above passages we are told that Paul used "reason" (διαλεγομαι), a word which indicates the concept of intellectual stimulus and even debate.[2] Paul additionally attempted to "persuade" (πείθω) his hearers to accept the truth and many did respond this way. This word describes the attempt to change a person's mind by the application of reason and also involves endeavoring to prevail in the discussion by winning them to one's viewpoint.[3] Paul additionally "alleged" (παρατίθημι) the truthfulness of Christianity, a word indicating the use of argumentation and proof.[4]

By these and other ways Paul argued for the truthfulness of the Christian message. His discussions were not simply verbal gymnastics, however. He was presenting key evidences by this method. Two evidences, in particular, were used most often. Messianic prophecy was used mainly with Jews, building on the basis of Old Testament Scripture.[5] The resurrection of Jesus was used with both Jews and skeptics.[6]

We could provide other examples of apologetics being used as an integral part of presenting the truthfulness of the Christian message. Such instances can be found both in Paul (Acts 13:16–41; 24:24–25; I Cor. 15:1–20) and in other places in the New Testament (Heb. 2:2–4; II Peter 1:16–21; I John 1:1–3 are examples).

---

[2]Acts 17:2, 17; 18:4, 19; 19:8–9; 24:25; see Vine, *An Expository Dictionary of New Testament Words*, volume III, p. 252. See also A. T. Robertson, *Word Pictures in the New Testament* (Six volumes; Nashville: Broadman Press, 1930), volume III, p. 267 for example.

[3]Acts 17:4; 19:8; see Vine, *Dictionary*, vol. III, p. 179. See also Robertson, *Word Pictures*, vol. III, p. 296, for example.

[4]Vine, Ibid., Volume I, p. 47.

[5]See Acts 13:23, 33–35, 40–41; 17:2–3; 18:4–5; 26:22–23; cf. 17:17; 18:19.

[6]See Acts 13:30–39; 17:30–31; 26:23, 26.

Also noticeable are New Testament examples where we can see a contrast in styles between directly preaching or teaching the gospel and using evidences. Even more interesting are instances where this contrast takes place in the ministry of one person, meaning that different styles were used depending on the occasion and audience. We see this contrast in Jesus' ministry between His discussions with the rich young ruler (Mark 10:17-27) and Nicodemus (John 3:1-15) and His usage of evidences with John the Baptist's disciples (Luke 7:18-23) and with His own disciples (Luke 24:36-43; John 20:19-20, 26-29; Acts 1:3). Peter's messages in Acts likewise show contrasts (cf. Acts 2:14-41 with Acts 10:34-44).[7]

Several conclusions may be drawn here, especially with regard to Paul's witnessing strategy. Initially, it was shown above how Paul and his companions went to various places in order to communicate the gospel. They possibly witnessed most frequently in synagogues, but also confronted people on a river bank, in jail, in a marketplace, at Areopagus, and in a lecture hall. Where people listened, Paul spoke.

Next, in addition to preaching and witnessing, Paul utilized various apologetic approaches in presenting the gospel, depending on the audience. With sympathetic audiences of Jews and God-fearing Greeks, it was noted above that Paul most frequently used fulfilled messianic prophecy from the Old Testament and the resurrection of Jesus. With skeptics such as those at Areopagus, Paul reasoned from other grounds, although he still used the resurrection as the chief evidence.[8] His goal in both instances

---

[7]In both of Peter's messages here, he uses the resurrection as an evidence, but it appears to be stressed less in the case with Cornelius.

[8]Again, a choice is not being made as to any particular apologetic methodology. The point here is that various approaches were used in the early church and are still needed today.

was to present Jesus as the Messiah who came to preach salvation to man. Additionally, attesting miracles were also performed.[9]

Another aspect concerns Paul's usage of different witnessing methods in order to present the gospel, such as preaching or proclaiming,[10] disputing or arguing,[11] or simply by normal conversation.[12] Again we find the method adapted to the audience.

Lastly, in whatever place Paul and his companions were, whether they used preaching and witnessing or evidential approaches and with each of the various methods used, the Holy Spirit blessed the message. As a result many heard the gospel and believed. Perhaps the key here is that Paul adapted himself to his hearers. He became "all things to all men" so that as many as possible would receive the gospel (I Cor. 9:19-23).

At any rate, it is hardly possible to claim that the early church did not perceive the importance of apologetics. Rather, evidences such as Old Testament prophecy and Jesus' resurrection were often used to validate the early Christian messages and presentations of the gospel.[13] Likewise, we have already pointed out the importance of using an evidential basis today as well.

## The Holy Spirit and Apologetic Systems

From the foregoing it is evident that the Holy Spirit made use of various approaches in order to present the gospel in

---

[9]For some examples of such attesting miracles, see Acts 14:3, 10.

[10]For instance, see Acts 13:5, 38; 15:36; 17:18, 23.

[11]See footnotes 1-5 above.

[12]See Acts 16:13; 17:19 for a couple of instances.

[13]Even critical scholars admit the early church's interest in using evidences to back its claims, For just a sampling of these instances, see Bultmann, "New Testament and Mythology," *Kerygma and Myth,* p. 39; *Theology of the New Testament,* volume 1, p. 27: Marxsen, *The Resurrection of Jesus of Nazareth,* pp. 125, 169; Bornkamm, *Jesus of Nazareth,* pp. 184-185.

the days of the early church. It is true that we stressed evidential approaches more. But as mentioned already, this is simply because of the nature of this work as a whole and because more people doubt the validity of apologetics than they do the direct preaching or teaching of the gospel. But we wish to make it plain that we also recognize the full validity of direct presentations of the gospel with little or no actual evidential treatment.

From this analysis we can also conclude that various techniques may be used by the Holy Spirit today. In many instances a simple presentation of the gospel is all that is needed to bring a person to trust Christ, because the Holy Spirit prepared that person's heart, making him ready to accept the gospel. In other cases, there may be a need for an extensive evidential basis before faith is exercised.

It is for this reason, as we asserted in the Introduction, that the apologetic presented in this book is not to be viewed as an exclusive way of presenting the gospel to modern man. Since the choice of approaches depends on the leading of the Holy Spirit according to such factors as the audience and the occasion, many methods are possible.

Neither is this system to be taken as an exclusive evidential approach to presenting the claims of Christianity. Again, various evidential approaches are also possible and we must be open to the Holy Spirit's guidance as to which is the most appropriate one under the conditions. It is also very possible to mix portions of various evidential approaches. But in all of this, the Holy Spirit must be viewed as the One who should be doing the leading.

In other words, we are acting incorrectly if we use an evidential approach with someone who is prepared by the Holy Spirit for a direct presentation of the gospel. In fact, the use of evidences may even harm that individual by bringing doubts to his mind which might not be there. Likewise, it is inappropriate simply to present the gospel and walk away from one who needs some serious questions answered, thinking we have done our jobs. Here we should present the evidences along with the gospel. Again, many cases are not so explicitly in need of any one approach by itself. Perhaps a combination approach is needed.

A point of caution is necessary here. We must point out that *no apologetic approach is a substitute for presenting the gospel.* It may be that a person refuses to hear the gospel before certain questions are dealt with. It is also possible that in various encounters we may not be able to present the actual plan of salvation because of extenuating circumstances. In such cases, evidences can still be a good preparatory step, such as in "sowing the seed" for a future presentation of the gospel. However, we must never think that a strong defense of the Christian message is a substitute for presenting the message itself. Acceptance of the way of salvation is a key goal of apologetics.

For these reasons, when we are contrasting a straightforward presentation of the gospel with an evidential approach, this is *not* a contrast between presenting the gospel and not presenting it. As we just concluded, salvation should be presented whenever possible according to the leading of the Holy Spirit. Rather, the difference concerns the usage of evidences along with giving the gospel.

With such options, it is important that we realize the crucial place which the Holy Spirit plays in apologetics. We must be sensitive to His leading or we may endeavor to use improper methods in presenting the Christian message.

This brings us to an additional caution. *No amount of reasoning can ever cause a person to trust Christ and His message of salvation apart from the Holy Spirit.* This is because unbelievers are simply not conditioned to the things of God and they do not understand them. The sin nature causes man to be blinded (I Cor. 2:14). Additionally, Satan affects unbelievers and causes them not to see the truth (see Eph. 6:12). Since the only means of overcoming such problems is God's power (II Cor. 10:4), we conclude that only the Holy Spirit can bring a person to salvation, simply because such an achievement is an act of God. All of our reasoning may even bring someone to an intellectual belief that our facts are correct *without* having them respond positively to Christ.

Therefore, the leading and teaching of the Holy Spirit is indispensable in apologetics. Since evidences are never a substitute for presenting the gospel, we must allow Him to lead us in the proper choice of witnessing and apologetic methods. We must be sensitive to His will. No argument can lead anyone to trust the Lord for salvation apart from the work of the Holy Spirit, for this is the work of God. This should further teach us to be submissive and allow Him to prepare the person's heart and bring them to receive Christ through our testimony. But the chief credit belongs to the Holy Spirit, for it is something we cannot do by ourselves.

## Evidences and Faith

Before concluding this chapter, we will address ourselves briefly to the relationship between evidences and faith. It is apparent from our study of Paul's method that there is essentially no conflict between the work of the Holy Spirit and apologetics.

Before an individual can exercise faith in Christ's Person and message, he must have exercised his reason in at least a preliminary form in order to understand the plan of salvation. In other words, faith is placed in Christ because of our previous knowledge of the gospel plan. Such knowledge is of course not exhaustive, but involves an understanding of the prerequisites of salvation.[14]

---

[14]For a more indepth study of the relationship between faith and reason, see Habermas, *The Resurrection of Jesus: A Rational Inquiry,* pp. 60–80. For another

With this basis, we may state that, speaking philosophically, our evidences are not proven 100 percent.[15] As we have done in this work, we can only speak in terms of probabilities.[16] Accordingly, faith must act upon these probabilities. Thus, the Scriptures present excellent evidences for the Christian faith, but such apologetic endeavors are not the same as philosophical proof. We must walk by faith and not be sight, which is what proof would be (II Cor. 5:7). Without faith we cannot please God (Heb. 11:6).

Perhaps an illustration will help here. When we get into a car to travel, we are often at least implicitly aware that there is a certain chance that we will be involved in an accident. Yet, we do not judge the probability of getting to our destination safely and then take only that percentage of our body into the car! Obviously, faith must act on these probabilities so that our whole body gets into the car. Faith does what the reason could not.

So too in Christianity, one must also decide on the evidence as prompted by the Holy Spirit. Some need very little evidence beyond judging that what they understand of God's action in Christ is worthy of belief. Others require more evidence. This is why various approaches are needed for different people. At any rate, faith acts on the knowledge and does what the reason could not. Reason comprehends the facts, but only faith appropriates them personally. Without the faith, all we have is intellectual assent, not salvation.

---

good discussion of this relationship, see John R. Stott, *Your Mind Matters* (Downers Grove: Inter-Varsity Press, 1973).

[15]Again, this is speaking from a philosophical angle. Believers can claim certainty by the witness of the Spirit (Rom. 8:16) and can *know* they are true Christians (I John 5:9-13).

[16]In this book, even such terms as *demonstrate* are a reference to validating a view according to probability. We have not used the term *proof* with our arguments simply because we are speaking in terms of probabilities.

Therefore, evidences may prompt faith. However, we should never endeavor to make evidences such that they are the same as sight. Remembering the examples of Thomas, we should be careful what we demand for our belief. Jesus pronounced a blessing on those who have not seen, but yet believe (John 20:26–29). Faith must act on the probability of the knowledge (not on sight-proof), thereby trusting God and His plan of salvation (Heb. 11:6).

## Conclusion

We have shown that various approaches are necessary in communicating the Christian message, according to the leading of the Holy Spirit. To repeat a question which we asked in the Introduction, how is this book to be used in the light of these conclusions? There we suggested two uses for this work, which we will expand only briefly here.

First, believers often need their own faith strengthened. Like John the Baptist in the gospels (Luke 7:18–23), believers sometimes have serious questions, too. Evidences often help to reassure us of the trustworthiness of the Christian faith, which we have already accepted. But once again, we should not demand evidence to the point of complete proof. With this qualification, our belief can be significantly assisted by such knowledge.

Second, such an evidential approach can also be used with unbelievers and especially with skeptics. Thus, in becoming "all things to all men," those who need strong evidences before accepting the Christian message may at least be confronted by the rationality of the gospel. Hence, as suggested in the Introduction, this apologetic might be used when a more evidential approach is needed. Perhaps, by the convicting power of the Holy Spirit, they may even be persuaded to exercise faith in Christ's Person and message.

Paul presented the gospel at Areopagus to skeptics who sneered at the Christian message (Acts 17:18-19, 32). Yet he did not give up but continued to make his case, even by citing Greek sources which were accepted by the philosophers. These sources, in turn, agreed with Paul's words (v. 28). Thus, by using these principles of agreement which were accepted by the skeptics, he showed that his message should also be accepted. His crowning demonstration was provided by Jesus' resurrection (vv. 30-31). As a result, some believed (v. 34).

In a similar way, many of the arguments in this book were also especially constructed for use with skeptics who likewise not only reject Christianity, but who also reject Christian foundations such as the inspiration of Scripture. Thus, we showed in Chapter 1, for instance, how the resurrection of Jesus can be affirmed as a historical fact even when using skeptical principles.

This is also why there are so many citations of skeptical and critical scholars in this book. The object here was not only to critique such positions, but also to show how even skeptical scholars accept certain important principles. As such, this might be a further incentive to the critic to examine these arguments more closely. At any rate, it is important to note that the systems of these skeptics are not being adopted or accepted here.

Another point to be stressed is that a key motive in this book has been to demonstrate that the Bible is the written Word of God. As such it serves as an infallible basis for Christian theology and living. As indicated in Appendix 2, it can be quoted and utilized as God's message to a fallen world. It both refutes world views which are contrary to it and presents God's revelation of the Christian theistic world view.

Therefore, we conclude that the apologetic system presented here may be used when a more evidential approach is needed. This may be either to strengthen the faith of believers or to convince unbelievers and skeptics by the power of the Holy Spirit.

Some of these assertions and principles are presented and developed here for the first time, to the knowledge of this author. It is our hope that they might even be used along with other systems for the best possible presentation of the Christian message.

Having finished our apologetic, we will give a final illustration of it as follows:

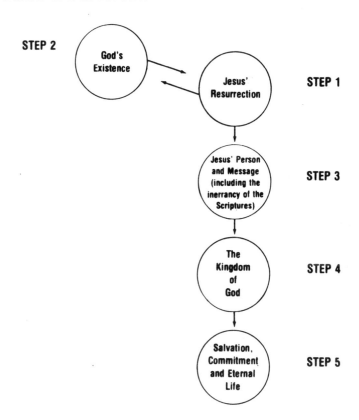

# A Bibliography

Anderson, J. N. D. *Christianity and Comparative Religion.* Downers Grove: InterVarsity Press, 1970.

Ayer, Alfred Julius. *Language, Truth and Logic.* New York: Dover Publications, Inc., 1946.

Barth, Karl. *Church Dogmatics.* Edited by G. W. Bromiley and T. F. Torrence. Thirteen volumes. Edinburgh: T. and T. Clark, 1961.

Bayly, Joseph. *The View From a Hearse.* Elgin: David C. Cook Publishing Company, 1969.

Berkouwer, G. C. *Studies in Dogmatics.* Translated and edited by Jack B. Rogers. Thirteen volumes. Grand Rapids: William B. Eerdmans Publishing Company, 1975.

Blüh, Otto and Elder, Joseph Denison. *Principles and Applications of Physics.* New York: Interscience Publishers, Inc., 1955.

Bonhoeffer, Dietrich. *The Cost of Discipleship.* Translated by R. H. Fuller. Second edition. New York: The Macmillan Company, 1959.

Bornkamm, Günther. *Jesus of Nazareth.* Translated by Irene and Fraser McLuskey with James M. Robinson. New York: Harper and Row, 1960.

Brightman, Edgar Sheffield. *A Philosophy of Religion.* New York: Prentice-Hall, Inc., 1946.

Brown, Raymond E. *Jesus: God and Man.* Milwaukee: The Bruce Publishing Company, 1967.

————. "The Resurrection and Biblical Criticism" in *Commonweal*, Novemeber 24 (1967): pp. 232-236.

————. *The Virginal Conception and Bodily Resurrection of Jesus.* New York: Paulist Press, 1973.

Bruce, F. F. *The New Testament Documents: Are They Reliable?* Grand Rapids: William B. Eerdmans Publishing Company, 1960.

Brunner, Emil. *Dogmatics.* Translated by Olive Wyon. Philadelphia: The Westminster Press, 1952.

Bultmann, Rudolf. *History and Eschatology: The Presence of Eternity.* New York: Harper and Row, Publishers, 1957.

————. *Jesus Christ and Mythology.* New York: Charles Scribner's Sons, 1958.

————. "New Testament and Mythology" in *Kerygma and Myth.* Edited by Hans Werner Bartsch. New York: Harper and Row, Publishers, 1961.

————. *Theology of the New Testament.* Translated by Kendrick Grobel. Two volumes. New York: Charles Scribner's Sons, 1951, 1955.

Burrows, Millar. *An Outline of Biblical Theology.* Philadelphia: The Westminster Press, 1946.

Clark, Robert E. D. *The Universe: Plan or Accident?* London: The Paternoster Press, 1961; reprinted by Zondervan Publishing House, 1972.

Cox, Harvey; Pannenberg, Wolfhart; Burkholder, Lawrence. "A Dialogue on Christ's Resurrection" in *Christianity Today,* volume 12, number 14, 12 April 1968, pp. 5-12.

Cullmann, Oscar. *The Christology of the New Testament.* Translated by Shirley C. Guthrie and Charles A. M. Hall. Revised edition. Philadelphia: The Westminster Press, 1963.

Denney, James. *The Death of Christ.* Edited by R. V. G. Tasker. London: The Tyndale Press, 1951.

Dodd, C. H. *The Parables of the Kingdom.* London: Nisbet and Company, Ltd., 1936.

Donnelly, John. Editor. *Logical Analysis and Contemporary Theism.* New York: Fordham University Press, 1972.

Filson, Floyd V. "Resurrection" in *Dictionary of the Bible.* Edited by James Hastings, revised edition by Frederick C. Grant and H. H. Rowley. New York: Charles Scribner's Sons, 1963.

Flew, Anthony. "Theology and Falsification" in *New Essays in Philosophical Theology*. Edited by Anthony Flew and Aladair MacIntyre. New York: The Macmillan Company, 1955.

Fuller, Reginald H. *The Formation of the Resurrection Narratives*. New York: The Macmillan Company, 1971.

_____. *The Foundations of New Testament Christology*. New York: Charles Scribner's Sons, 1965.

Geisler, Norman. *Christian Apologetics*. Grand Rapids: Baker Book House, 1976.

_____. *Philosophy of Religion*. Grand Rapids: Zondervan Publishing House, 1974.

Gill, David. "Radical Christian: Rethinking our Financial Priorities" in *Right On,* volume 12, number 6, February–March (1976): p. 12.

Habermas, Gary. "Hume and Inerrancy" in *Philosophical Roots of Biblical Errancy*. Edited by Norman Geisler. Grand Rapids: Zondervan Publishing House, 1980.

_____. *The Resurrection of Jesus: A Rational Inquiry*. Ann Arbor: University Microfilms, 1976.

Harris, R. Laird. *Inspiration and Canonicity of the Bible*. Grand Rapids: Zondervan Publishing House, 1969.

Holland, R. F. "The Miraculous" in *Logical Analysis and Contemporary Theism*. Edited by John Donnelly. New York: Fordham University Press, 1972.

Hume, David. "Miracles" in *Enquiry Concerning Human Understanding*. From *Hume on Religion*. Selected and introduced by Richard Wollheim. London: Collins Clear-Type Press, 1963.

Kierkegaard, Søren. *Attack Upon "Christendom"*. Translated by Walter Lowrie. Princeton: Princeton University Press, 1968.

Ladd, George Eldon. *I Believe in the Resurrection of Jesus*. Grand Rapids: William B. Eerdmans Publishing Company, 1975.

_____. *The Pattern of New Testament Truth*. Grand Rapids: William B. Eerdmans Publishing Company, 1968.

Lewis C. S. *Miracles*. New York: The Macmillan Company, 1947.

Lightner, Robert P. *The Saviour and the Scriptures*. Grand Rapids: Baker Book House, 1978.

Lovett, C. S. *Death Made Easy*. Baldwin Park: Personal Christianity, 1964.

MacDonald, William. *True Discipleship*. Kansas City: Walterick Publishers, 1962.

Marxsen, Willi. *The Resurrection of Jesus of Nazareth*. Translated by Margaret Kohl. Philadelphia: Fortress Press, 1970.

Metzger, Bruce M. "Inspiration" in *Dictionary of the Bible*. Edited by James Hastings, revised edition by Frederick C. Grant and H. H. Rowley. New York: Charles Scribner's Sons, 1963.

Moltmann, Jürgen. *Theology of Hope*. Translated by James W. Leitch. New York: Harper and Row, Publishers, 1967.

Nicole, Roger. "Redemption" in *Christian Faith and Modern Theology*. Edited by Carl F. H. Henry. New York: Channel Press, 1964.

Orr, James. *The Resurrection of Jesus*. Grand Rapids: Zondervan Publishing House, 1965.

Pannenberg, Wofhart. "Dogmatic Theses on the Doctrine of Revelation" in *Revelation as History*. Edited by Wolfhart Pannenberg. New York: The Macmillan Company, 1968.

———. *Jesus—God and Man*. Translated by Lewis L. Wilkins and Duane A. Priebe. Philadelphia: The Westminster Press, 1968.

———. *Theology and the Kingdom of God*. Edited by Richard John Neuhaus. Philadelphia: The Westminster Press, 1969.

Paterson, William P. and Gilmour, S. MacLean. "Jesus Christ" in *Dictionary of the Bible*. Edited by James Hastings, revised edition by Frederick C. Grant and H. H. Rowley. New York: Charles Scribner's Sons, 1963.

Ramm, Bernard. *A Handbook of Contemporary Theology*. Grand Rapids: William B. Eerdmans Publishing Company, 1966.

Randall, John Herman, Jr. *The Making of the Modern Mind*. Revised edition. Boston: Houghton Mifflin Publishing Company, 1940.

Reichenbach, Bruce. *The Cosmological Argument: A Reassessment*. Springfield: Charles C. Thomas, 1972.

Riggenbach, Eduard. *The Resurrection of Jesus*. New York: Eaton and Mains, 1907.

Robertson, Archibald Thomas. *Word Pictures in the New Testament*. Six volumes. Nashville: Broadman Press. 1930.

Robinson, James M. *A New Quest of the Historical Jesus*. London: SCM Press Ltd., 1959.

Robinson, John A. T. *Exploration into God*. Stanford: Stanford University Press, 1967.

Rowe, William. *The Cosmological Argument*. Princeton: Princeton University Press, 1975.

Schleiermacher, Friedrich. *The Christian Faith*. Edited by H. R.

Mackintosh and J. S. Stewart. Two volumes. New York: Harper and Row, Publishers, 1963.

Schweitzer, Albert. *The Quest of the Historical Jesus.* Translated by W. Montgomery. New York: The Macmillan Company, 1968.

Stein, Robert H. "Was the Tomb Really Empty?" in the *Journal of the Evangelical Theological Society,* volume 20, Number 1, March (1977): pp. 23-29.

Stoner, Peter W. and Newman, Robert C. *Science Speaks.* Chicago: Moody Press, 1968.

Stott, John R. W. *Your Mind Matters.* Downers Grove: InterVarsity Press, 1972.

Strauss, David Friedrich. *A New Life of Jesus.* No translator given. Two volumes. London: Williams and Norgate, 1879.

Swinburne, Richard. *The Concept of Miracle.* New York: The Macmillan Company and St. Martin's Press, 1970.

Taylor, Vincent. *The Atonement in New Testament Teaching.* Third edition. London: The Epworth Press, 1963.

————. *The Gospel According to St. Mark.* London: Macmillan and Company Ltd., 1963.

Tillich, Paul. *Systematic Theology.* Three volumes. Chicago: The University of Chicago Press, 1951, 1957, 1963.

Trueblood, David Elton. *Philosophy of Religion.* Grand Rapids: Baker Book House, 1973.

Van Buren, Paul M. *The Secular Meaning of the Gospel.* New York: The Macmillan Company, 1963.

Verwer, George. *Come! Live! Die! The Real Revolution.* Wheaton: Tyndale House Publishers, 1972.

Vine, W. E. *An Expository Dictionary of New Testament Words.* Four volumes. Old Tappan: Fleming H. Revell Company, 1966.